*The Mosque*

# *The Mosque*
## The Heart of Submission

R USMIR  M AHMUTĆEHAJIĆ

F ORDHAM  U NIVERSITY  P RESS
N EW  Y ORK   2006

The Abrahamic Dialogues Series, No. 3
ISSN 1548-4130

Library of Congress Cataloging-in-Publication Data

Mahmutćehajić, Rusmir, 1948–
    The mosque : the heart of submission / Rusmir
Mahmutćehajić.— 1st ed.
        p.    cm. — (The Abrahamic dialogues series,
    ISSN 1548-4130 ; no. 3)
    Includes bibliographical references.
    ISBN 0-8232-2584-4 (hardcover : alk. paper)
    1. Mosques.    2. Salat.    3. Islam—Essence, genius, nature.
I. Title.    II. Series.
BP187.62.M34    2006
297.2—dc22        2005032422

Printed in the United States of America
07 06  5 4 3 2 1
First edition

*In memory of my friend*
*Harald de Meyenburg*

# Contents

*Foreword* William C. Chittick

This is a remarkable little book. As I read it through I was astonished at Dr. Mahmutćehajić's ability to reformulate classical positions of Muslim thinkers and spiritual teachers in fresh and original ways. Despite his use of a nondenominational language, he is completely in line with the Islamic intellectual tradition founded by the Qur'an and the Prophet and echoed down through the ages in the writings of numerous sages and saints. Nowhere do we meet a simple rehash of old ideas, but rather a fresh and ongoing rediscovery of the riches of prophetic wisdom.

Those seasoned in Islamic thought and spirituality will find old friends appearing in new guises on every page. Those familiar only with the distorted picture of the Islamic tradition that is the stock-in-trade of the media will no doubt wonder where these teachings are coming from. Reading through the book they should gradually be able to understand that the basic source is simply a pure heart, free of the trammels of prejudice and ideology and open to the discovery of God's wisdom in the beauty of creation, scripture, and tradition.

Dr. Mahmutćehajić is well known for his writings on Bosnia and in particular for his attempts to delineate ways in which the religious communities there can reestablish the amicable relations that they had in the past. People familiar with those writings will have noticed that he has a rare sensitivity toward the deeper dimensions of religion in general. This little book brings that sensitivity to bear on the most profound questions of human life and destiny.

In fulfilling Dr. Mahmutćehajić's request that I write a foreword, it occurred to me that a bit of background might be useful for those unfamiliar with the Islamic tradition. Christians in particular may suppose that "the Mosque" is the Islamic analogue of the Church, the mystical body of Christ. But the "mosque" has no similar connotation for Muslims, and to think it did would be to commit the same sort of error that one does when one refers to Islam as "Mohammadanism" on the model of Christianity.

Throughout Islamic history, the mosque has played a variety of roles in diverse cultures and communities, but it has never taken on the central role of the Christian Church, not least because there is no priesthood in Islam and hence no room for an institutionalized mosque under an official hierarchy. Or, to phrase this differently, every Muslim is his or her own priest and typically performs most religious obligations in the home, so every Muslim home is in fact a mosque. The function of the mosque is dispersed throughout society and indeed, throughout the natural world as well. In a well-known saying the Prophet remarked that he was given six things never given to any previous prophet, one of which was that the entire face of the earth was designated as his mosque.

The English word mosque derives from the Arabic *masjid* by way of French, Italian, and Spanish. *Masjid* means literally place of prostration (*suj*). Prostration designates putting the forehead on the ground as is done twice in every cycle of the salat, the Muslim ritual prayer. Given that Muslims perform seventeen cycles of prayer in observing the commandment to pray five times a day, the act of prostration is done at least thirty-four times a day by practicing Muslims. There are additional, voluntary salats that Muslims may perform, and in reciting the Qur'an, reading certain verses obligates the believer to perform a prostration.

The Qur'an's use of the word prostration prefigures some of the points that Dr. Mahmutćehajić brings out in his essay. Significant, for example, is the manner in which the Qur'an associates its meaning with that of *islâm*—submission or surrender to God. Prostration clearly offers a striking symbol for surrendering to God's will. But notice that in the Qur'an, both *islam* and prostration, like worship (*'ibâda*) and being a servant (*'abd*), have two basic sorts: compulsory and voluntary. The compulsory sort derives from our created nature:

> To Him is submitted everything in the heavens and the earth. (3:83)
>
> To God prostrate themselves everyone in the heavens and the earth, willingly or unwillingly. (16:49; cf. 22:18)
>
> There is no one in the heavens and the earth that does not come to the All-merciful as a servant. (19:93)

Thus *islâm,* prostration, and servanthood are qualities of every created thing, since all creatures serve their Creator by the very fact of being creatures. A second sort of *islâm* pertains specifically to the prophets and all those who follow prophetic guidance. The Qur'an calls Abraham, the Apostles of Jesus, and various other pre-Islamic figures "Muslims," that is, possessors of the quality of *islâm* or submission.

The Qur'an also tells us that pre-Islamic peoples performed the salat (though few Muslim theologians would imagine that the salat of previous communities took exactly the same form as that instituted for the followers of Muhammad), and "prostration," in the Islamic understanding, is an essential part of salat. If the following verse only speaks of "some" in referring to People of the Book (Jews and Christians), it is for the self-evident fact that not every member of a religious community lives up to its ideals.

> Some of the People of the Book are an upright nation, reciting God verses in the watches of the night, *prostrating* themselves, having faith in God and the Last Day, bidding to honor and forbidding dishonor, vying with each other in good works—those

are among the worthy. And whatever good they do, they will
not be denied the just reward of it. (3:113–14)

The act of prostration plays an important role in the story of
Adam's creation. Recall that God commanded the angels to prostrate
themselves before Adam, because God had created Adam to be his
vicegerent and had taught him "all the names" (2:30–34). The angels
did so, but Satan refused. Satan was not one of the angels—who by
definition never disobey God—but a jinn, made of fire rather than
light. He had entered the ranks of the angels through pious works, but
these were not enough to save him from pride and envy. When he
refused to obey God's command, God said to him, "What prevented
you from prostrating yourself when I commanded you to do so?" He
replied, "I am better than he. You created me of fire, and You created
him of clay" (7:12). "I will not prostrate myself to a mortal whom
You created out a clay of molded mud" (15:33).

Satan, then, is the leader of all those who are too proud to prostrate
themselves at the command of God. These are the *kuffâr*—the unbelievers, the ungrateful, those who cover over the evidence of their created nature and deny their debt to God.

And when they are told, "Prostrate yourselves to the All-merciful," they say, "And what is the All-merciful? Shall we prostrate ourselves to that which you command us?" (7:12)

Prostration also plays an important role on the Day of Resurrection. When Adam and his children are gathered on the plain of the
Mustering and God descends to them, they will be commanded to
prostrate themselves. But those who did not prostrate themselves dur-
ing their lifetimes will not be able to do so in death.

On the Day the leg is bared and they are summoned to prostration, but they cannot. Humbled shall be their eyes, and abase-
ment shall overcome them, for they had been summoned to
prostration when they were whole. (68:43)

The inability of unbelievers to prostrate themselves at the resurrection indicates a life lived in error and denial, for the mode of one's

resurrection is nothing if not the fruit of one's actions. The final act of disobedience demonstrates worthiness for hell, and hell is simply the distance from God—who is reality, awareness, goodness, mercy, love. The cause of distance is clinging to one's own illusions and individuality. "Nay, on that Day they shall be veiled from their Lord" (83:15).

In contrast, those who prostrate themselves at the resurrection acknowledge their insignificance in the face of God Reality. The fruit of this acknowledgment is to be taken into God's proximity, a nearness that the Qur'an calls "paradise." Thus the Qur'anic command addressed to every human self, "Prostrate yourself, and draw near" (96:19).

Dr. Mahmutćehajić's book, like most texts on Islamic spirituality, circles around the issue of *tawhîd*, that is, the assertion of God's unity formulated most succinctly in the first testimony of faith, "(There is) no god but God." Unusually for Islamic texts, however, Dr. Mahmutćehajić speaks of God as "the Self," and he contrasts the Self with "the self," that is, the individual human soul. If few scholars have used this sort of language to express *tawhîd* in English, this may have something to do with the fact that authors of books on Hinduism have a near monopoly on the use of the term "Self." Nonetheless, it should not be thought for a moment that Dr. Mahmutćehajić is simply borrowing the terminology from another tradition. Rather, he is using appropriate Islamic language to make a point that is made constantly in the texts, but not with the usual Arabic word that is translated as self.

In Arabic, the basic reflexive pronoun is *nafs*. The Qur'an often uses *nafs* in the standard way, that is, to refer back to any noun or pronoun. But it also uses the word with the definite article and independent of a noun to which it refers, and in these cases the word designates the human self as a generic notion. Translators of the Qur'an typically render the word in this sort of context as soul. Thus, in Arabic, *al-nafs* means "the (human) self," and it would be very odd indeed to use the expression to refer to the divine Self. Rather, when one wants to refer to God's Self, one uses other terms, most commonly *dhât*, usually translated as "Essence" and contrasted with the divine attributes, which are the names and qualities that give news of the Essence. This word *dhât* is also used on occasion as a reflexive pronoun.

This is not to say that it is improper to use the word *nafs* for God, given that the word can refer to any noun. One Qur'anic example of such usage is especially interesting because it sets up precisely a point about *tawhîd* that Dr. Mahmutćehajić is stressing. Moreover, it does so through the mouth of Jesus, and it echoes Jesus' own version of the formula of *tawhîd* in the Gospel: "Why do you call me good? No one is good but God alone" (Mark 10:18). The Qur'anic verse I have in mind is this:

> And when God said, "Jesus son of Mary, did you say to the people, 'Take me and my mother as gods, apart from God?'"
> He said, "Glory be to You! It is not mine to say what I have no right to say. If I indeed said it, You know it, for You know what is in my self, but I do not know what is in Your Self." (5:116)

Given that *dhât* is not a Qur'anic expression and *nafs* is rarely used in reference to God, is there any other word used by the Qur'an that approximates Dr. Mahmutćehajić's use of "Self"? Indeed there is, and that is simply the personal pronoun "I" (*ana*). Especially telling are the three instances in which the Qur'an employs this word in the formula of *tawhîd* "There is no god but I" (16:2, 20:14, 21:25). Ibn 'Arabi calls these three instances "*tawhîds* of the *anâya*," that is," of the I-ness," though one could as well translate *anâya* as "the Self." All three of these instances, it should be noted, address the issue of the universality of revelation, the fact that God says "I" to each prophet, thus setting up a certain divine subjectivity and even exclusivity for the specific message.

The first of the three verses sums up the content of God's message to all prophets: "God sends down the angels with the spirit of His command upon whomsoever He will of His servants: 'Give you warning that there is no God but I, so fear Me!'" (16:2). The attribute of "godfearing" or "god-wariness" is the highest virtue to which a human being can aspire and is much discussed in the texts. It might be defined as the attitude of "prostration" before God in every thought and every act. Its importance is highlighted in the Qur'anic verse "Surely the noblest of you in God's eyes is the most godfearing of you" (49:13).

The second *tawhîd* of the Self is mentioned in the story of Moses and the Burning Bush. The Qur'an does not cite the pregnant Biblical version of God's words, "I am that I am," but tells the story like this:

> When he came to the fire, a voice cried, "O Moses! Verily I am your Lord. Take off your shoes. Verily you are in the holy valley, Towa. I have chosen you, so give ear to what is revealed: Verily I am God. There is no god but I. So worship Me, and perform the salat to remember Me." (20:11–14)

Notice that once again the implication of the *tawhîd* of the Self is that the human self must devote itself to God through "worship," which is to be his servant in the manner in which he requests. The primary way in which one serves and worships God is to perform the "salat," which can be understood as the specific form of worship instituted by a given revelation.

The third instance of the *tawhîd* of the Self is especially telling, because it epitomizes the Islamic understanding of religion and illustrates the Qur'anic position that all the prophets (traditionally said to number 124,000) came with essentially the same message—*tawhîd* and worship: "We never sent a messenger before thee except that We revealed to him: 'There is no god but I, so serve Me'"(21:25). Let me conclude by quoting Ibn 'Arabî's commentary on this verse:

> In this verse God mentions "worship," but no specific practices, for He also said, "To every one [of the prophets] We have appointed a Law and a way" [5:48], that is, We have set down designated practices. The periods of applicability of the practices can come to an end, and this is called "abrogation" in the words of the learned masters of the Shariah. There is no single practice found in each and every prophecy, only the performance of the religion, coming together in it, and the statement of *tawhîd*. This is indicated in God's words, "He has laid down for you as Law

what He charged Noah with, and what We have revealed to thee [O Muhammad], and what We charged Abraham with, and Moses, and Jesus: 'Perform the religion, and scatter not regarding it'" [42:13]. Bukhârî has written a chapter entitled "The chapter on what has come concerning the fact that the religion of the prophets is one," and this one religion is nothing but *tawhîd*, performing the religion, and worship. On this all the prophets have come together.[1]

Stony Brook, 4 September 2004

# Introduction

Man exists in space and time. At any space and time we can turn in any number of potential directions—but none can bring us fulfillment, for nothing that happens to us is enough in itself. But all boundedness in space and time has the potential to direct us toward the Boundless, that which lies beyond all boundaries. As each place receives us, each moment leaves us behind: we are travelers in search of an outer world and an innermost self that constantly eludes our grasp. As long as they elude us, we are guests, not prisoners, in a world of signs which, near and far, all point toward the Destination.

And every voice, every sign, merges with that Destination, in celebration and praise of the One who manifests Himself through the myriad signs in the outer world and the inner self. The process of self-realization in the world is a struggle, a ritual at the threshold of the forbidden, the inviolable.[1] The inviolability of the forbidden, and our relationship to it, means that we can never define ourselves, but also that we have no existence beyond what defines us, beyond the boundaries within which we exist.

Oneness is the source and purpose of all the myriad signs. But Oneness lies hidden, and cannot be reduced to any one sign, nor to all of them combined. It is this same Oneness which forms man's innermost reality. In discovering and opening ourselves toward the unity of everything in the outer world, we can come to recognize at any time and place that everything stems from that Oneness, and exists for it. Whatever our attitude toward this Center, it remains inviolable. It cannot be destroyed or altered.

But we cannot achieve self-realization without the teachings that arise from it and are one with it, without worship at the threshold of the unattainable, or without the virtue which is inseparable from both. Whenever we actualize the center of our being, we become a guest at the Table which was sent down so that God might manifest Himself. This Table is also the world's *masjid*, its mosque, for there is nothing that does not show submission to God. Any resistance to this universal reality stems merely from the delusion that the boundaries of phenomena are impassable.

This essay discusses the relationship between Oneness, as the innermost center of the human self, and its signs in the outer world—in the unspoiled natural world, and in all the diverse houses built and maintained in order to call the Name of God.

Most of the text was written between 8 and 12 October 2003 in Fátima in Portugal. An abridged version was presented on 12 October at the Congresso de Fátima on "The Present of Man—The Future of God: The Place of Sanctuaries in Relation to the Sacred"; the remainder was completed between 13 and 15 October, also in Fátima.

*The Mosque*

# 1. The Self and the self

The Complete Self cannot be Complete, and free itself from conceal-ment, without becoming manifest—and It can become manifest only in the contingent self. In becoming manifest, It speaks of Itself as Completeness in the contingent. Both the Self and the self speak—the Self to the self, but also vice versa; and as there are a myriad selves, all of these speak to one another.

Speaking involves listening. A speaker has a right to be listened to; this is determined by the listener openness, willing or otherwise, toward the speaker's message. By allowing speakers this right, listen-ers oblige speakers to listen to them too. Hence the relationship be-tween I, the self who speaks, and the other, the self who listens, is one of rights and obligations on both sides. This means that I and my other are interdependent: no one of us can lay claim to completeness.

I, selfhood, and others, alterity, both need dialogue in order to be-come aware of our boundedness. The self and the other are both con-tingent, and nothing in their relationship can attain Completeness, though Completeness is everyone Other. The relationship between self and other is one of language, and hence one of boundedness, but also one defined by the Alterity that lies beyond all bounds. The recognition that I who speak am contingent, and that what I say must also be so, is the precondition for taking the contingent other to be my listener. In so doing, I testify to my contingency, but also to the possibility of transcending it, of drawing closer to Completeness. Thus I, the self, can demand my right to be listened to and, by speaking, become indebted to my listener—which also implies avoiding making any judgments of my listener. Hence the speaker recognizes every other to be a contingent manifestation of the Complete.

Perfection is present in every self, but this does not mean that every self is perfect. But in recognizing its own contingency, the self becomes able to orient itself toward Perfection, and becomes indebted to the Self.

The self, in turning toward the Self at any point in space and time and seeking out its primal nature, recognizes a Messenger as its "fairest example." This must be an act of free will. The only evidence for such a decision is the virtue of the Messenger and those who follow him, and the changed lives of those who hear his call. The Messenger's self is affirmed through total submission, through non-selfhood where the Self reveals Itself: it is this that makes him a Messenger. He is of the Complete, and manifests the Complete: the perfection that is present everywhere finds full expression in him.

Hence the Messenger is the path and the gateway to the Complete, as expressed in the testimony "I testify that there is no god but God, and I testify that the Praiser[1] is His servant and messenger"—the declaration that the Self has revealed Itself through my self. The Complete Self can only become manifest in the whole of creation—that is, in every separate sign in all the worlds—and through the contingent self, which is the sum of every separate thing in all the worlds. The Self is manifest in every self, though in a myriad different ways. All that exists does not equal the Self, nor is it without the Self: each self is a manifestation, an image of the Self. Through this act of manifestation, the self, the world and humankind praise the Self.

The Complete Self is both Light and Praise. As such the Self both sheds Light and offers Praise. The universe and human beings receive this Light and Praise, and they are in turn illuminated and praised to their fullest. In the Messenger, this Praise and Light come together perfectly, and so he too is Illuminated and praised. This is human plenitude. In the act of bearing witness to Oneness, the Messenger knows that all Light and Praise belong to God, Who is illuminated and praised by His Own Being and by all creation. Therefore, the Messenger is the bringer of Light and singer of Praise.

The Self is both absent and present in the world and in man. The Self's presence is revealed in Its will, and Its absence in human forgetfulness and opposition—that is, in will which has turned toward non-Self. The latter cannot, however, prevail over the Will of the Self, for although the Self allows for insubordination and opposition, It subordinates itself to no other: truth cannot subordinate itself to lies, nor can lies become truth. If the Self were to accept that there were anything other than Itself, the perfection of the order underlying all that exists would be shattered.[2]

The self, therefore, lies between Self and non-Self. Since the Self is completeness, it bears all potential in its oneness, including non-Self. The Self is Goodness and Knowledge, but non-Self is the void. Human intellect relates to goodness, and forgetting to the void. Whenever the self is oriented toward anything other than the Self, it acknowledges non-Self, the void without the Self and Completeness.

Since, at any point in space or time, the self lies between these two extremes, it is defined by its orientation toward the good, which means remembering and affirming its primal nature; or toward evil, which means forgetting the oneness of the Self. The fact that the Self contains all potential, including non-Self, is realized through creation. The Self's goodness is what compels It to give Itself—that is, to become manifest through creation. But though creation is the manifestation of the Self, of Goodness, by coming into being it also brings about disconnection—that is, evil.

Evil is any principle of disconnection from the Good, any move by the created toward non-Self, whereas good is any move toward the Self; and moving toward the Self means moving away from non-Self. In the whole of creation there are countless multitudes of levels, of which some are closer to the Self and some further from It. The world of direct experience, or "this world" is counterbalanced by "the other world" as its higher reality. As such, "the other world" is better—that is, closer to primal goodness.[3] However, no level of existence is governed by the principle of non-Self: at any level, everything is determined by how the Self reveals itself through that level's signs.

And nothing is without purpose:[4] everything was created to praise the Creator, and the act of praising gives reality to all phenomena. But when the self and the phenomena within its ken become disconnected from Knowledge, they become implicated in evil, for they deny the Completeness of the Self and turn away from It toward non-Self. Yet they can never attain non-Self, for the Self encompasses all things. Hence no time or place can reach a state of total forgetting. Evil can never have the last word

## 2. THE SELF THAT SPEAKS

The words "Verily I am God; there is no god but I; therefore serve Me,"[1] which are both Divine and human, testify both to the Complete and to the contingent. In that the words come from the Complete, they assume a listener who is meant to hear them; and in being heard, the words become the listener's. Listener and speaker, being two, form a differentiation of the Complete within Itself. Yet they cannot be the Complete: they merely manifest the One through duality. Because It has no associate, the Complete can only be revealed through duality. That which is Hidden does not "become" that duality by revealing Itself in duality—duality is merely Its manifestation. Thus, if the self that hears and receives is not Completeness, then the world in which and in contrast to which the self exists cannot be Completeness either. The self and the world are the speech or manifestation of the Complete, which they can neither condition nor annul. The opposite of the Complete is the void; and the world and the human individual both exist in the relationship between the Complete and the void. When they associate themselves with the Complete, they are its servants, its manifestation, and Completeness itself. But when they associate themselves with the void, they are nothing. The Complete is oneness, and nothing can constrain it or fully comprehend it. All potential lies in the Complete, even the potential to be perceived relative to the void, to nothingness. Through this act of revelation—that is, manifestation or creation—its love makes it both hidden and open, far and near, one and many, combined and separate.

Whenever the self defines itself, it orients itself beyond the limits of multiplicity and separateness toward Oneness as first principle. The earth and the heavens were a single clod;[2] all people derive from a single soul;[3] all people were a single community;[4] and all will return to its Creator.[5]

When the Self manifests Itself, Its undifferentiated names become differentiated in all their infinite multiplicity. Every phenomenon in the world has its own name or names that derive from the hidden and the distant, from oneness and togetherness. When all the names come together, stillness manifests itself in motion, oneness in multiplicity, closeness in distance, and so on. Creation comes full circle in the human individual, where the Self speaks through the self, and both become speaker and listener.

When the self recognizes the unboundedness of the world as its image and as the manifestation of the Self, it attains the state of servitude in which Completeness can link the self who serves with the Self Who Speaks: "Recite: in the Name of thy Lord, who created."[6] As we recite, as we distinguish between the myriad names which the self knows in the outer world and gathers into itself, creation reveals itself to be the speech of the Creator about His Oneness. And in reciting, we praise all the manifestations of Oneness: "Nothing is, that does not proclaim His praise."[7] Self-realization means gathering all praise of the Self into one's self, and becoming Its perfect revelation. Whoever sees the Self in this way sees the Truth,[8] for perfect submission to the Praised transforms the self into the praiser, and the Self becomes the door to the Truth.[9]

The Self always knows the self, but the self can never know the Self.[10] Only the Self can know Itself. Yet the self can discover itself as reality only in the Self. This potential is the Compassion of the Self: we may call on God by different names, but every call knows His Names to be the most beautiful.[11]

The Self calls to the self, and expects to be heard, expects to be called on in return. The Self is both hidden and manifest, both far and near, both one and separate, and It speaks to the state of submission made reality by the Self: "And when My servants question thee concerning Me—I am near to answer the call of the caller, when he calls to Me; so let them respond to Me."[12] With these words, the self as actor also testifies to the Self as recipient. The relationship becomes a two-way potential for speaking and listening, which subtracts nothing from the Complete, and the world becomes a place which reveals that there is no self but the Self.

If the Self is the Lord, the self is His servant. There can be no lordship without service, nor service without lordship. In this, both find wholeness, and faith in one another. As both Lord and servant swear to be faithful to one another, the relationship between them is, quite literally, one of confidence, of mutual trust:

> We offered the trust to the heavens and the earth
> and the mountains, but they refused to carry it
> and were afraid of it; and man carried it. Surely
> he is sinful, very foolish.[13]

By nature, therefore, we are beings who know all the Names,[14] and who have accepted a trust unlike anything else on earth and in heaven, making ourselves into a world within but distinct from all the other worlds, into an interface between the worlds and God. This interface is the human heart: through it, the whole of existence becomes separated and gathered together again—separated by the revelation of Oneness in creation, and gathered together as it returns to that same Oneness. The trust thus offered opens a range of possibilities for those who receive it: at one extreme is the slide into nothingness, through violence to and ignorance of themselves and the world; at the other lies perfect submission to the Self as revealed to the self.

As an interface, we constantly straddle a border, a border which defines our self: our physical existence on the one side, and our guiding principle on the other, in the realm of the inviolable. Only through ritual and struggle can we connect our presence on one side with our orientation toward the other, the inviolable, the complete.

## 3. THE WORLD

God is both hidden and open, one and many, and therefore the self can turn toward Him from any level of memory; this testifies to how all names are encompassed by the Sacred Name, and by His Mercy which, as He says, encompasses all things.[1] The Lord says: "Verily, My mercy predominates My wrath."[2] And the Prophet says: "God created a hundred mercies on the day He created the heavens and the earth, each mercy of which would fill what is between the heaven and the earth. Of these He placed one mercy in the earth. Through it the mother inclines toward her child, and the birds and animals incline toward each other. When the Day of Resurrection comes, He will complete those mercies with this mercy."[3]

Living between mercy and Mercy, we have no excuse for forgetting Him. The presence of mercy, always and everywhere, testifies to the manifestation of the Divine. The myriad phenomena whose manifestations make up the whole of existence are imbued with this mercy. Only in the fullness of Mercy can we attain that realization which we merely sense in our earthly presence.

The world reveals its Creator, whose "love to be known" is His mercy. His Oneness contains all possibilities, which he reveals through the myriad signs in the outer world and the depths of the self.

The self also contains our ineradicable debt to Reality. By manifesting itself in creation, Reality has neither lost nor gained anything; It remains what It is both before and afterwards. Manifestation or creation is wholly indebted, in its inwardness and outwardness, to Reality. The relationship between the created and Reality is one of debt, with the repayment of the debt the actualization of createdness in the Truth.

The universe and the human self and the revealed word are all merely the expression of that mutuality between Reality, to Which the debt is due, and createdness, which is indebted. The memory of this debt is the link between the Creator and existence; it is held at the center of the human self, which was created to seek a union with Oneness. Even if the debt be forgotten or repudiated, it can never vanish or be cancelled, for the whole of existence testifies to the nonexistent.

God says, through the Messenger Muhammad, the Praiser: "I was a Hidden Treasure, so I loved to be known. Hence I created the creatures that I might be known."[4] The hidden and the revealed are opposites, but God's potential brings them together.[5] Creation is revelation, and thus stands in opposition to the hidden. The link between them is the love that lies in the hidden.

What is known is filled with love for the hidden, for no self can find fulfilment in the revealed. It seeks the Self—the Hidden One Whose face is concealed by seventy thousand veils of light.[6] As one removes these veils, one discovers one's self, through a process that is the very condition for the self's existence. The self exists for as long as it can remove the veils: when all the veils are removed, there is no more self, no more existence. Hence the veils are the signs or places through which the Self reveals Itself. They are subordinate to the Self, because they have nothing other than the Self. They are Its servants, and in serving they realize themselves. Everything that is in the heavens and on earth submit to Him;[7] all that is in the heavens and the earth praises God.[8]

This act of submission, willing or otherwise, shows that everything in existence is imbued with the Truth.[9] Existence has no reality of itself: existence is "the debt" which every phenomenon owes to Reality. When this debt is denied, in terms of its self the phenomenon becomes a corruption or distortion of its sign, its name—it becomes an idol, a sign that has lost its connection with the "hidden treasury." But when the debt inherent in the relationship is accepted, the whole of creation glorifies and praises non-existence, praises the Hidden. This is the *sajda*, the prostration in worship, performed by all that exists:

> Hast thou not seen how to God prostrate all who are
> in the heavens and all who are in the earth,
> the sun and the moon, the stars and the mountains,
> the trees and the beasts, and many of mankind?[10]

The world is thus the place where everything that is not the Self proclaims its reality by way of debt and submission. The world is the revelation of the hidden; but as the hidden is revealed, it gains and loses nothing. The whole of existence and all its individual signs depend on the hidden which they reveal; and they bow down, together and separately, in worship before the Face that they both veil and reveal.

The world is one vast mosque or "place of prostration"[11] and every phenomenon in the world owes a debt to God by bowing down before Him. In the human self, all that is differentiated and dispersed through the world is gathered together again to become oneness. Moreover, we have a covenant with God on the basis of trust, of "confidence." Hence the human self, as the Perfect Man or his potential, is the reflection of the greater world and is thus also a mosque; as Jesus says, "Destroy this mosque, and in three days I will raise it up."[12] Raising up the *masjid* spoken of here means affirming and proclaiming that the center of the human self is open to the Complete, and forbidding that it be reduced to the non-Complete.

Since all selves are imbued with Reality, at all times and places they have the newness of Divine creation. They are separate, being in time and space; but they are also connected, for they have no reality without Reality. Wherever it may be, the self is oriented toward the Face of the Complete. And so the Self and the self can look one at another and see itself through the other, though they are both contained in and connected to Oneness. As Creator and Complete, God shows mercy to the self. As for the self, at any time and place it has the potential to declare its face to be the image of the Face; and through the act of prostration before the Face, to achieve the nothingness and so to confirm itself in the Reality.

Humankind's original, supreme potential is to exist in a world that acknowledges its Creator through all its being and all of its signs. This state of being includes Oneness as the center of all existence—as all the signs and the human heart, which is the very center of Oneness, say loud and clear. Both centers, self and Self, form a boundless duality that proclaims and confirms oneness.

But if the external center is repudiated, they become separated from each other and are left alone in the darkness. The self then comes to forget the Self, even though its potential to remember remains unbroken. But the self's mere presence in the world is no longer enough to retain and strengthen this potential: hence the need for teachings, worship and virtue. The teachings show the self that there is no god but God, and worship orients the self toward the boundary between the world of duality and its Center that lies in Oneness. When the self has accepted the teachings and knows itself to be part of a procession around a single Center that we know as the Inviolable, it must then accept its duty to be humble and generous. This can all be achieved at any time or place. There is no excuse for forgetting and idleness in this world of time and space, as God tells us from the perspective of the Day of Judgment:

> Say: "My servants who believe, fear your
> Lord. For those who do good in this world
> good, and God's earth is wide."[13]

# 4. HUMANKIND

As it was God who offered us the covenant based on "confidence," His obligation is the greater. There is no ignorance or violence in God: He is Complete. This means that His trust in the covenant that results from the offer is also Complete. The fact that this covenant with God is a relationship of choice, of confidence—rather than one of submission and servitude without free will, as is the case with "the sun and the moon, the stars and the mountains, the trees and the beasts"— necessarily leaves us prone to ignorance and violence.

And yet we have the potential to bring our will into compliance with the will of God by entering this covenant of mutual trust with Him, so that one and the same trust may be made reality in His image, as God says through the Prophet Muhammad, the Praiser:

> My servant draws near to Me through nothing I love more than that which I have made obligatory for him. My servant never ceases drawing near to Me through supererogatory works until I love him. Then, when I love him, I am his hearing through which he hears, his sight through which he sees, his hand through which he grasps, and his foot through which he walks.[1]

Thus, when our will conforms to the will of God, we are the complete image of our Creator. Nothing in that image resists the Creator; everything reflects and bears witness to Him. This makes us into His mosque, the locus where the Divine will finds expression. In being His mosque, we know every sign in the outer world to be a message which speaks its contents, a missive for us to read from the One in Whose image we are made:

> We shall show them Our signs in the horizons and
> in themselves, till it is clear to them
> that it is the truth.[2]

This "We" dissolves the duality of hidden and revealed, showing that the opposites are really one—We in I and I in We. Here a triad may be seen: We, the signs in the outer world, and the signs in the self. The "We" shows the signs to "them," so that they may know that "He is the Truth." "We" is merely another way of saying "He, the Truth": first as active principle, the one who shows, and then as recipient, that which is shown.

The signs "in the horizons" are the macrocosm or outer world, and the signs "in themselves" are the microcosm or inner world. Since the macrocosm is also concentrated in every human self, it exists in a multitude of forms, though in the Self it is one and the same. Both the macrocosm and the human self reflect this other side of existence: this is the law of reciprocity, which shows how phenomena that are differentiated and visible correspond to the undifferentiated and invisible. The seeker's goal is to unite, in the Self, the three expressions of reality—God, macrocosm and microcosm, all three of which are mentioned in the verse quoted above. The conditional nature of the signs points toward the Complete; but when the seeker understands that there is no reality but Reality, he attains oneness.

God is Completeness—which means that all potential lies in Him, including non-Self. As soon as His hidden nature is revealed, existence becomes linked both to Self and to non-Self. The reality of every phenomenon lies in its link with Self, and non-reality in its orientation toward non-Self. The potential for both is what we know as free will.

Human beings can achieve self-realization insofar as their will freely conforms to the Will of the Self. Each new moment, however, can impose and undo this relationship, and our acceptance of this trust inevitably implies both remembering and forgetting. The world is never equal at any single point in time, and though we owe our reality to Reality, our will both helps and hinders our efforts to achieve self-realization through awareness of this debt. The stronger our awareness, the greater our submissiveness.

And the greater the submissiveness of the self, the more the signs in the outer world correspond to those in the soul, revealing Reality all the more clearly. Everything in the inner and outer worlds, and every work and deed of human invention and construction, becomes a legible sign in the Book of the world, of humankind and of revelation. Here, in the mosque, everything that has place and time in the world takes on its true being. And the mosque's purpose is to praise God by calling out His Name.

When multiplicity reveals Oneness, it becomes a Praiser—the servant, messenger and perfect image of the Praised. The Self testifies that the Praiser is the servant and messenger of Oneness in human image, for the Praiser stands in the "fairest stature"[3] as our most "beautiful example."[4] With this noble potential, the human being becomes the sum total of meaning in the world: "God made him a transcription comprehending everything in the macrocosm and all the names of the Divine Presence."[5]

The multiplicity of human selves confirms and proclaims the Oneness of the Self. This can only take place via that single Center which "loves to be known." This love finds its realization through creation. Once Oneness is differentiated into Self and non-self, into Creator and created, existence finds its realization in praise of the Creator, by which He becomes manifest in everything.

As we are the sum total of all creation, praise is our deepest and highest reality. When we attain perfection in praising, we become the perfect image of the Praised. Into this Completeness, the Praised sends down the Book. The Book is inseparable from the nature of the Praiser: his self is in the Book, and it is in him. The path toward this highest of human potentials begins at any time or place in our existence. When we stand upright in space and time as the recipient of the message, we orient ourselves toward the Praised. And the way passes through the gates of the exemplary Praiser.

> You have a good example in God's Messenger
> for whosoever hopes for God and the Last Day,
> and remembers God oft.[6]

# 5. THE BOOK

The universe is a table containing all of God's separate signs; these reveal the potential that lies in the hidden treasury of the Divine Self. Every sign is a manifestation of that Word which is one and the same, the Word which is in every sign and contains the whole of knowledge.

The Word was sent down by God into the human self, so that it might gather together everything that is separate in the outer world and open us to the unending current that confirms Oneness.

Thus God's Word, as manifested in all the diversity of creation, was reassembled in the innermost depths of the human self. Undifferentiated, the Word contains all the knowledge of the Self; but differentiated, it comprises all the signs revealed in the outer and the inner worlds. These separate signs form the book of Divine knowledge, which is Complete. We may recognize the invitation it contains or may deny it, as God's question in the Recitation indicates: "Didst thou not know that God knows all that is in heaven and earth? Surely that is in a Book."[1]

The fact that everything that exists is contained in this Book means that the whole of creation is nothing other than God's speech about Himself. This speech is undifferentiated in principle and purpose:

"Every term has a Book. God blots out, and He establishes whatsoever He will; and with Him is the Mother of the Book."[2]

The One God manifests Himself throughout the myriad worlds.
The separate signs of His manifestation are gathered together in the
human self, and through this process we know ourselves to be the sum
total of creation.

God sends His book down to us via His chosen messengers.
Though He is One, the messengers are many, each transmitting the
same message through different languages, teachings and rites. As
God says, "Every nation has its Messenger.[3] And "To every one of
you We have appointed a right way and an open road. If God had
willed, He would have made you one nation; but that He may try you
in what has come to you. So be you forward in good works; unto God
shall you return, all together; and He will tell you of that whereon you
were at variance."[4] "We have sent no Messenger save with the tongue
of his people, that he might make all clear to them."[5] "And of His
signs is the creation of the heavens and earth and the variety of your
tongues and hues."[6]

The ineffable name of God is revealed in a myriad names and attributes. The Word that is One and the same empowers a countless host
of words, as God says in the Recitation: "Though all the trees in the
earth were pens, and the sea—seven seas after it to replenish it, yet
would the Words of God not be spent."[7] The Word of God creates,
which means that it reveals. Through it, God reveals His love to be
known. The Word is ruler and judge, for He alone knows all things:

> With Him are the keys of the Unseen;
> none knows them but He.
> He knows what is in land and sea;
> not a leaf falls, but He knows it.
> Not a grain in the earth's shadows,
> not a thing, fresh or withered,
> but it is in a Book Manifest.[8]

The all-knowing Self, though revealed in and with the Book
through Speech, has its center in the Hidden. Since the human self

contains the whole of creation, our speech is a response to the knowledge about the Self which the signs in the outer and inner worlds have given us.

We, as the image of the Merciful, also have speech—which, in its supreme form, is the speech that the Creator has sent down to us from His treasury. Human language, therefore—the separate languages and language as a whole—gathers together all the manifest worlds and selves. The prophets, the messengers of the Self, are those who take all the worlds and selves into themselves. Their innermost essence, the goal of their creation, is the act of praise. They shape their whole self by the Book, and their entire nature becomes what has been revealed to them. The hidden, "inviolable" nature of their innermost self is nothing other than the hidden, "inviolable" nature of the Self. They bear witness that there is no god but God and that the Praiser is His Prophet. On receiving the Book, they teach themselves and others, and draw the line between evil and good.

The sole purpose of their learning and teaching is to raise the self so that it might regain its "fairest stature" within the Self. The self's supreme potential in the world lies in hearing, remembering and taking to heart the prophets' telling of the Book. Among the tellings recorded and experienced in time are the Torah, the Psalms, the Gospels and the Qur'an. These are distinct texts, but each carries one and the same message, which is to be found in all the other written and unwritten messages and experiences of the 124,000 prophets of God which the Praiser counted from Adam to himself. And these prophets bore two clear signs, the Book and the Balance, so they might bring justice to humankind.[9]

The Spirit that is Faithful and Holy instilled the Recitation in the Praiser's heart:[10]

> Even so We have revealed to thee
> a Spirit of Our bidding. Thou knewest
> not what the Book was, nor belief;
> but We made it a light, whereby We
> guide whom We will of Our servants.[11]

God has invited everyone, from first until last, to sit at the table of signs in the outer and inner worlds. By coming to know the signs, we come to know ourselves; and by knowing ourselves, we know our Lord. And this knowledge inspires and channels love toward the Hidden One, Who manifests Himself through the signs in the outer and inner worlds and in the books.

The table is sent down, and we are invited to sit at it. We cannot sit at this table without permission from the One who sends it down. We are expected—indeed required—to behave humbly, as guests at someone else table, for humility is our only debt to God.[12] Receiving, remembering and reciting His signs, "In the Name of God, the Merciful, the Compassionate," enables us to realize ourselves, for they are "with the truth." Turning toward these signs in the macrocosm reveals God's Face in our own face—the face of Him who has no other, and beside which all vanishes. Recognizing His signs in the macrocosm, the self or the book requires *sajda*, prostration, as an affirmation of His Oneness and Omniscience. All His Names and all His Words return to Him:

> And of His signs
> are the night and the day, the sun and the moon.
> Bow not yourselves to the sun and moon,
> but bow yourselves to God who created them,
> if Him you serve.[13]

# 6. DIGNITY

Humankind was created in "the fairest stature"—that is, in supreme uprightness or verticality. As created beings, our original nature wholly reflects the will of God. At the core of our selves we open ourselves to a meeting with that will, which means that our original uprightness is the unity of two wills, the Divine and the human—an inner unity that cannot be abjured. As the principle of all that exists, it is also the inviolable.

Thus joining ourselves to the inviolable is what makes us truly upright; and our upright stature enables us to transcend our createdness and enter into a covenant with the Creator, thus realizing our original and supreme potential:

> And when thy Lord took from the Children of Adam,
> from their loins, their seed, and made them testify
> touching themselves, "Am I not your Lord?"
> They said, "Yes, we testify"—lest you should say
> on the Day of Resurrection, "As for us, we
> were heedless of this."[1]

This testimony is a covenant based on trust. Its parties are the Complete Self, which is infinite, and the contingent self, which realizes itself only in and with the Self. Whereas the Self undertakes to determine the outcome of this covenant, the freedom of the self, of humankind, is contingent.

This freedom gives us four choices: to submit and believe (thus attaining sanctity); to ignore the knowledge at the center of our self (thus making the periphery central, and the center peripheral); to associate ourselves with the periphery (thus subordinating the world and others to ourselves); or to change our behavior depending on whom we are with (thus ignoring the fact that God is omnipresent: "Has thou not seen that God knows whatsoever is in the heavens, and whatsoever is in the earth? Three men conspire not secretly together, but He is the fourth of them, neither five men, but He is the sixth of them, neither fewer than that, neither more").[2]

The very question "Am I not your Lord?" implies a choice of answers: yes or no. In choosing to answer yes, we acknowledge that we are part of creation, and thus separate from the Complete. This separation, however, can be bridged by aligning our will with our knowledge and love for the Complete. Existence means that the Self reveals Itself relative to the non-Self.

But saying no, turning toward the non-Self, warps the will away from the Self, reducing love to one or other of its components, and knowledge to narrow-mindedness. Whenever the link with the Self is broken, we forget our debt to It. And as we forget, we inevitably abandon ourselves to non-Self and descend to the lowest of the possible planes of existence. But whatever depths we sink to, when we return we turn away from non-Self.

Whichever of the four possible choices we have made, the Spirit that God has breathed into us[3] remains at our primal core, a core which contains both the Lord's question and our answer.

And our very freedom to say yes or no is what makes us beings of openness, of receptivity. Our primal center constantly offers us the opportunity to seek redemption through the "right religion," the enduring debt[4] which one can settle by returning to God:

> So set thy face to the debt,
> a man of pure faith—God's original
> upon which He originated mankind.

There is no changing God's creation.
That is the debt; but most men know it not—
turning to Him.[5]

This debt, or religion, is present at the center of each individual. One of its expressions is the Lord's question, and the answer that we give. The answer can be given through different teachings which follow different paths, but always involves submission to God, the possibility of calling out to Him by His Name which is central to our human status. Knowing His most beautiful names and using them to summon Him means finding self-realization in beauty.

And "God's original"—the unalterable, inviolable and forbidden center—is the human heart, which in its oneness and sameness remains open to all the names and words which reveal the Hidden. Our answer "You are!" to God's question echoes His "I am!" for both testify to the oneness of the human and the Divine will in the act of creation.

The Messenger says: "The hearts of all the children of Adam are like a single heart between two of the fingers of the All-merciful. He turns it wherever He desires. O God, O Turner of Hearts, turn our hearts toward obeying Thee!"[6]

When our hearts are turned toward the Creator, we stand upright in our fairest stature, as creatures who gather together and speak the Names of God. Our dignity as human beings consists of the potential to turn toward God and to accept His command that we must repel evil with good.[7] And also the potential to bear in mind that we must answer to an all-knowing Judge for every atom of good and evil that we do,[8] and that the noblest among us are those who are most aware of their origins and their ultimate accountability.[9]

Through that center, the self is able to draw infinitely near to the Self. Its dignity is therefore inviolable, by dint of the Spirit within it. The body is an extension of that center and surrounds it, and thus it too is inviolable. And there can be no society, no community if their center does not show both aspects of the same dignity.

Human dignity is also inviolable among and with respect to other people. The dignity of the body that manifests the Spirit is protected vis-à-vis others by clothes. Only in lawful marital relations may these clothes be shed, for husband and wife are each other's garments.[10] And since the house is an extension of the body, another of its garments, it is also inviolable.[11]

Husband and wife share a single inseparable inviolability, and their sexual relations bear witness to unity as the reason and purpose of love. This is because, at every time and place, each self has the potential to prostrate itself before God.

Since the world is created in submission to God's will, it is in complete order. There is no discord, and nothing in the heavens and earth was created in vain. We humans are the only creatures who can enter into the primal covenant, through the free will bestowed on us by that act of trust. Any betrayal of this covenant is a denial, wilful or otherwise, of the self's original testimony as given in our answer "You are!"

Hence the dignity of the center, of the body, of our presence among other people and in the world demands that we preserve and confirm the workings of the world—for these are inseparable from the inviolable center.

# 7. ARRIVAL AND RETURN

All that exists comes from God. The whole of creation and every individual thing has God as its Other; but God has no other of His own.[1] Hence every phenomenon perceives Him as both infinitely close and infinitely far. He is God, the One; and in that oneness He is the All-faithful,[2] loving and knowing. His love demands to be known, and He is flow and change. Every moment of time, every atom of matter proclaims His oneness, although He begets not, nor is He begotten.[3]

Everything that exists is a confirmation of Oneness. We humans are the sum of all existence, and as such we return to God: "Surely we belong to God, and to Him we return."[4] In this valley of existence we reflect all of creation; in us we protect and keep sacrosanct the place of submission, the *masjid* or mosque where we receive that primal knowledge which is identical to love.

This sacrosanct *masjid* is the human heart, which is open to flow and change, redirecting all the knowledge it stores to show us that God is both near and far. The potential at our center tells us that He is near, and the fact that the whole universe cannot contain Him shows that He is far. The human individual is a microcosm of the whole, whereas other beings merely form its parts. Each human being has all the attributes of the macrocosm, whereas all other beings display only some of these attributes. Other beings follow a predetermined path, which cannot be changed by act of will. Human beings have no predetermined path, for they share the indeterminacy of all creation. Hence our ultimate meaning is a mystery, just as our Creator is a mystery.

This openness orients humans toward infinity—as shown by the fact that the center of the world and the self is sacrosanct, is forbidden, is under interdiction. This interdiction sets certain places and times apart from others, and makes them both accessible and inaccessible; it draws a boundary through the world and the human self, and thus forms part of holy teaching, worship and virtue. This interdiction allows us to gain self- realization by striving toward what lies beyond the boundary—toward the source and haven of ourselves and the world. Self-realization means transcending duality—indeed, all transcendence is transcendence from duality. But where there is duality, there is struggle: hence the realization that there is no self but the Self can only be attained through struggle.

In our struggle to transcend duality, we travel toward the Farthest Mosque, only to discover that the farthest, the othermost and the last is also the nearest, the first and the primal. This act of discovery makes us the guests of the One who manifests Himself in all of creation; we are invited to His table, which is sent down from heaven. As we travel the path from self to Self, we become ever more aware that the signs in the self and the outside world tell us how He has made all the worlds into a table, a table at which we are invited to sit: "And He has subjected to you what is in the heavens and what is in the earth, all together, from Him. Surely in that are signs for a people who reflect."[5]

Jesus says: "For I proceeded forth and came from God; neither came I of myself, but He sent me."[6] And to this he added, "If I honour myself, my honour is nothing."[7] The human self finds reality only in praise of the Self. The Praiser is the one who is first to submit himself; and thus God commands the Praiser: "Say: 'I have been commanded to serve God making my debt His sincerely; and I have been commanded to be the first of those that surrender.'"[8]

The supreme reality of the Praiser lies in his servitude, debt and submission to the Lord, as Jesus confirms: "The servant is not greater than his Lord; neither he that is sent greater than He that sent him."[9]

Accepting the ultimate marginality of the human self and the centrality of the Divine Self means acknowledging that all of creation has a purpose, that the Praiser is God's servant and messenger, and that the innermost essence of every messenger is to be a path to the Praised One. "He that receiveth me receiveth Him that sent me,"[10] said Jesus. To receive the world as signs means receiving and gathering into one's self the knowledge that they reveal. In order to receive, we need to submit; but once we do so, we can read the signs in the outer world and come to understand ourselves. And by knowing the One who calls and sends us, we become His steward, His guest in the world. And in receiving the One we know to be ever-present behind the veils of existence, we come to love Him and desire to see ourselves in Him, to draw close to Him in the person of the Praiser. The Praiser's duty is to tell us, "If you love God, follow me, and God will love you, and forgive you your sins."[11] As Jesus also says: "He that hath my commandments, and keepeth them, he it is that loveth me: and he that loveth me shall be loved of my Father, and I will love him, and will manifest myself to him."[12] Obedience to the Divine commandments and submission to God's will, in other words, opens human beings to God's mercy, compassion and generosity.

One might see the unending flow of creation as consisting of two waves: one which descends toward us, and one which returns upward. Hence the universe may be symbolized by a circle consisting of two arcs—one of descent and one of ascent. The first arc descends from the prime Intellect, and the second rises from the human body. We are at the lowest point of the second arc, deep in the valley of existence, but we can see the whole circle and hence realize its beginning in ourselves.[13]

All human selves are one and the same; and however many outward manifestations they may have, they still lie "between two of God's fingers." Here, "between two of God's fingers," is our home, our *masjid*. Because our return, our ascent, starts from the arc's lowest point, reaching the highest point means uniting ourselves with our source, the active/prime intellect.

In all the infinite differentiation between their signs, the worlds testify to the farness and incomparability of God: "Like Him there is naught."[14] To understand Him requires Him to be similar and accessible. But as God is all-knowing and all-powerful, we in our unknowingness and powerlessness relate to Him as the ultimate Other: all of God's attributes belong to Him alone. But though His Self is not finite, the selves to which and through which He speaks are finite. They can express the Ineffable: this is their secret, and this is what makes them guests in the world and in themselves. And since God is with them wherever they are,[15] He is their home and their host. To Him they turn, and to Him they return; He is closer to them than their jugular vein.[16]

# 8. SPACE

The whole of existence, all the heavens and all the earth, forms a space for the Self to reveal Itself. But although space and time have no reality without the Self, they are not the same as the Self.

The Self is goodness, but also infinite potential. Its creation out of goodness also testifies to non-Self, that which is not the first principle. All phenomena in space are signs which reveal the Hidden but add nothing to it. Individually and collectively, they have no reality other than Reality. Their condition is one of ultimate submission and servitude.

The world is a house in which Peace reveals itself, in which the Lord receives His servants. All things return to God, and the revelation of what He has kept hidden begins as Spirit and ends as Humankind.

As Spirit, the whole of existence is undifferentiated potential. This potential becomes differentiated in the world and then reassembled in the human individual. This enables us to climb from the depths of the valley of creation toward the mountaintop, which is where the Self begins to reveal Itself.

The Intellect reveals the light of its message in the lesser world of signs—that is, through the prophets and their books. These books both gather together and differentiate, as instructed by Intellect; and they both descend and ascend.

Wherever we may be, the indestructible center that is open to the Spirit is always with us. When the Spirit firmly prevails over the material world in this center (that is, the heart), we can testify that all the signs in space and time belong to that Spirit. The Holy Mosque in the outer world corresponds to the center, the heart that is one and the same, in every human self. This duality of outer and inner serves to confirm Oneness as the source and destination of all things. And thus, wherever we may be, we are called to turn toward the *masjid*:

> Turn thy face toward the Holy Mosque; and
> wherever you are, turn your faces toward it.[1]

By dispersing signs throughout the outer worlds in a pattern reflected in the human self, God selects the places and times where his *We* can show the various aspects of the fact that "He is the Truth." And thus He says, through His Messenger:

> Glory be to Him, who carried His servant by night
> from the Holy Mosque to the Further Mosque
> the precincts of which We have blessed,
> that We might show him some of Our signs.
> He is the All-hearing, the All-seeing.[2]

By turning toward the Holy Mosque and knowing that all the signs in the Valley are images of the Mountain whose summit is the Spirit, we are carried through the night of existence to the Further Mosque. For only when the duality of outer and inner is resolved, only when we turn toward the Holy Mosque and attain that purity of heart which is the sole principle of all existence, can we perceive all the signs in the outer world and the inner self, together with their link to the Creator.

Existence, from the prime Intellect to the furthest frontier with non-Self, comes full circle and becomes revealed. All that is sent down is sent upwards again. The farthest is revealed in the nearest. Every point in space and time surrenders itself to the revelation of Oneness. Thus, by describing his state as one of liberation and perfect servitude, where all self-rule is surrendered, the Messenger reveals that God cannot be described in terms of material additions and imperfect metaphors.

"By night," that is, within the darkness of the bodily blights and the natural attachments, since ascent and advance take place only by means of the body. "From the Holy Mosque," from the station of the heart. The heart is too holy for the circumambulation of the idolaters—the bodily faculties—and the commission of their indecencies and mistakes. And it is too holy for the pilgrimage of the animal faculties, whether the beastly or the predatory. The twin evils of their going to one extreme and the other extreme are exposed, since they are naked of the clothing of virtue. "To the Further Mosque," which is the station of the spirit, the furthest from the corporeal world. This takes place through the witnessing of the self-disclosures of the Essence and the "glories of the Face." [ . . . ] Each station can be put in order only after the traveler advances to what lies beyond it. Then you will understand that His words, "that We might show him some of Our signs," refers to the witnessing of the divine attributes. Although viewing the self-disclosures of the attributes takes place in the station of the heart, the Essence described by those attributes is not witnessed to perfection in majesty and beauty until advance to the station of the spirit. God is saying, "that We might show him the signs"of Our attributes inasmuch as they are ascribed to Us and We are witnessed through them and appear in their forms. "He is the Hearing": He hears his invocations in the station of the inmost mystery, seeking annihilation. "The Seeing": He sees the strength of his preparedness, his turning his attentiveness toward the locus of witnessing, his being attracted toward Him through the strength of love and the perfection of yearning.[3]

From any given time to the next, the human self finds itself in a different place. This constant shift of time and place can only be seen by the pure heart, which proclaims, "He is God, One, God, the Ever-lasting Refuge, who has not begotten, and has not been begotten, and equal to Him is not any one."[4] This is because He is constantly at work.[5] At any time and place the world is a mosque, and so are we.

God's Name is mentioned in the houses and above the animals, in us and above us. Since everything is of God, the sole purpose of every time and place is to proclaim His Name. If this is forgotten, then places and times are ascribed to non-Self, which means denying that all of existence is sent down from Oneness and returns to It. By calling out His Names, we acknowledge that all things are from God.

# 9. TIME

"I am the Hidden Treasure" means that the divine I is eternal and infinite. "I love to be known, hence I created the creatures" tells how time and space reveal the eternal and infinite. Since the human self is the sum of everything in the universe, it gathers time and space into itself.

All phenomena confirm the names that God taught Adam. The phenomena which reveal these names exist in time and space. They disclose what is hidden by determining the places and times for prayer, almsgiving, fasting and pilgrimage as expressions of our submission. At any time, anywhere in the world can be a place for God to reveal Himself.

Outwardly, we turn toward the world and its signs; inwardly, toward our heart, our inviolable center. The former leads to what is distant, the latter to what is close. When the turning is total, so is the closeness. Turning toward the Holy Mosque means testifying in our hearts that all the signs are His.

Prayer is determined by His speech in the universe and in the Book. When we pray, we ground ourselves in space and absorb the time when all the world sings the praises of its Lord: "His is the praise in the heavens and earth, alike at the setting sun and in your noontide hour."[1] The position and movement of our bodies, and the speech and silence of our mouths, turn toward His Face: "When you have performed the prayer, remember God, standing and sitting and on your sides. Then, when you are secure, perform the prayer; surely the prayer is a time prescription for the believers."[2] God commands: "Be you watchful over the prayers, and the middle prayer; and do you stand obedient to God."[3] The times ordained are daybreak and dusk,[4] the beginning and end of the day,[5] that is, before sunrise and sunset;[6] just after the sun has passed the zenith;[7] after sunset;[8] and at night.[9] In addition, God decrees a communal act of worship just after the sun has passed its zenith on the sixth day of the week.[10]

Prayer is the way to join oneself with the cosmos in praise of God. It strengthens our feeling of indebtedness and the need to clear our debt by giving. Prayer and almsgiving, therefore, are two facets of our participation in the submission of the worlds.[11] Although specific times are set aside for prayer, its consequences last for all time: "Surely God bids to justice and good-doing and giving to kinsmen; and He forbids indecency, dishonour, and insolence, admonishing you, that haply you will remember."[12] "And whatever good you expend is for yourselves, for then you are expending, being desirous only of God's Face."[13]

Since all things are from God, and all things return to Him, giving confirms the declaration that there is no self other than the Self. Thus the dignity of createdness and return is confirmed at the center of the self: "It is not piety, that you turn your faces to the East and to the West. True piety is this: to believe in God, and the Last Day, the angels, the Book, and the Prophets, to give of one substance, however cherished, to kinsmen, and orphans, the needy, the traveller, beggars, and to ransom the slave, to perform the prayer, to pay the alms."[14] Hence almsgiving is an aspect of the virtue which confirms one's acceptance of the prescribed way and teaching as revealed by God. Here the Day of Judgment is what motivates all of time.

Giving confirms the reality of the self through its links with others. The depths of the self are inexhaustible. Giving depends on a recipient, whereas God is dependent on nothing and no-one. Hence fasting is another facet of submission, for then the self takes nothing from the outside world and thus bears witness to its center, into which God has breathed His Spirit. "And that you should fast is better for you, if you but know; the month of Ramadan, wherein the Recitation was sent down to be a guidance to the people, and as clear signs of the Guidance and the Salvation."[15] Fasting lasts all day, from the moment when the first rays of dawn can be discerned in the darkness of the night until nightfall.[16]

The declaration that there is no god but God and that the Praiser is His servant and messenger demands confirmation in prayer, which is inseparable from self-purification by almsgiving and fasting. The time for prayer is determined by the position of the sun in regard to the place where we are when we pray. When performing our ablutions and praying we face toward the Holy Mosque, the outward Mosque, to which our heart is attuned—that heart which is one and the same in all people and always lies between two of God's fingers.

In the month of Ramadan, fasting lasts each day from dawn to sunset, and from the first sighting of the new moon to its disappearance at the end of the month. Hence the sun is present in the self as the sign of Intellect, and the moon as its reflection in Reason,[17] in our ability to calculate.

The Holy Mosque toward which we face in prayer testifies to the duality of inner and outer, first and last. But God is one and only. Hence the pilgrimage to the Holy Mosque is a further expression of the testimony that there is no god but God. Both the time and place for the journey have been ordained by the Creator. "The first House established for the people was that at Bekka, a place holy, and guidance to all beings. Therein are clear signs—the station of Abraham, and whosoever enters it is in security. It is the duty of all men toward God to come to the House a pilgrim, if he is able to make his way there."[18]

Turning and traveling toward the Holy Mosque means striving for purity of heart in and beyond all change, in and beyond Reason and Intellect. God reveals to the Praiser: "They will question thee concerning the new moons. Say:'They are appointed times for the people, and the Pilgrimage.' " [19] "The Pilgrimage is in months well-known." [20]

The lunar and the solar year flow through and over one another. In them, everything constantly waxes and wanes, gains and loses strength, showing itself in the pure heart as the revelation of the hidden God.

Traveling toward the Holy Mosque or the Purified heart requires one to forego the pleasure of sexual intercourse and disputes, for awareness of God makes the best provisions. [21] Wherever and whenever people set out for the Holy Mosque as a sign of their journey toward purity of heart, "they shall come unto thee on foot and upon every lean beast, they shall come from every deep ravine that they may witness things profitable to them and mention God's Name on days well known over such beasts of the flocks as He has provided them." [22]

# 10. NATURE

The world, as the differentiation of His Names into multiplicity, is the place that reveals non-place. We are created in the image of our Creator, and placed on earth to be its stewards. But we too, being created, are just as subordinate as everything else in the outer world. This subordination lies beyond multiplicity, and hence is perfect potential. At source, ours is the fairest stature: we stand upright on the earth, pointing toward heaven. Our path is vertical and leads toward infinity. At its uttermost limits, human being encompasses both the Self and the non-Self, from Fullness to the void.

Our rule or stewardship of earth makes us responsible for the meaning of the earthly phenomena that are subject to us. They are signs that tell of Oneness; hence to deny them is tantamount to closing the gates of heaven, or denying the other face of phenomena: "Those that cry lies to Our signs and wax proud against them—the gates of heaven shall not be opened to them."[1]

Our purity, as the harmony of the inner self, is inseparable from the purity and harmony of the signs that are subordinate to us on earth. The earth's surface is where we can bow down with the world in prayer. Loving God and following His Messenger demands purity: "Truly, God loves those who repent, and He loves those who cleanse themselves."[2]

In so doing, we realize the whole of existence in ourselves. All of God's attributes are revealed in us, for we are the sum total of creation. To achieve perfection, the servant reverts to his primal nature— that of servitude, of total openness to God's overlordship. In submitting himself to this overlordship, the servitude of the Perfect Man is not sullied by impurity. Humanity means losing oneself and living in oneself. God says: "Be you securers of justice."[3]

And justice means knowing the right measure, without shortfall or excess. Knowledge of this kind is impossible without purity of self. Indeed, it is the purpose of human life to purify the soul and connect it with the light which sent it down. Purity of soul brings salvation by passing on and preserving in human experience what the Intellect has pledged.

The soul acts along a spectrum ranging from the purity and satisfaction of peace to the benightedness and temptations of evil. And God swears by this differentiation:

> By the soul, and That which shaped it
> and inspired it to lewdness and godfearing!
> Prosperous is he who purifies it,
> and failed has he who seduces it.[4]

The purity of nature is the image of the purity of the soul. Only from the purity of nature can the soul learn how nature is differentiated into an infinite multitude of signs which, individually and collectively, have their primordial origins in the hidden Treasury and are gathered together in the self.

The self manifests life, knowledge, power, will, sight, hearing, and speech, all of which are attributes of the Creator. The self brings these together in the heart, so that all that is differentiated in the outer world and the inner self can flow through its fullness. And here, in this oneness and sameness, lies the Treasury:

Naught is there, but its treasuries are with Us,
    and We sent it not down
    but in a known measure.
And We loose the winds fertilising,
and We send down out of heaven water,
then We give it to you to drink, and
you are not its treasurers. It is
We who give life, and make to die,
and it is We who are the inheritors.[5]

When the soul submits to the Spirit, the center of being gathers everything together out of differentiation and restores it to the oneness of the Treasury, and vice versa. But when the soul sets itself over the heart, when it does not submit to the Spirit, its aspiration to subjugate rather than submit makes its lusts unquenchable. "Had the truth followed their caprices, the heavens and the earth and whosoever in them is had surely corrupted. Nay, We brought them their Remembrance, but from their Remembrance they turned."[6]

Hence the purity of nature is one great mosque, the mirror of the heavens. Our status in nature makes us its stewards. But the purity of nature, though subordinate to us, directs us toward the infinity of heaven. By enabling us to transcend the twin options of descending into the depths of matter, as urged by the soul inclined to evil, and of moving to and fro along the surface, it frees us to move toward nonpotential and become complete submission.

We stand, therefore, in the mosque of the world which, by telling us of the world perfection, testifies that there is no self but the Self. We are in the world of which we are part, but we are also a window to the Complete. We are also here with the Book, which we are taught and which we learn.

Human perfection reveals itself in virtue—that is, in generosity and humility—and in the worldly skills of listening, speaking, writing and reading. We are creatures in whom all of creation, and thus every possibility of the Creator, is gathered together. We bear witness to this when we build a mosque in the image of the Mosque.

But the true mosque, as built by the Perfect Man, is made by manifesting the Self through our deeds. In this we only serve, as builders, guests and guardians. Every true mosque is a reflection of God love toward humankind, the love by which He sees and listens, and by which He works through us.

## 11. The Opening

The Divine I creates through the word and speaks through the act of creation. His undifferentiated word incorporates all names, and creation reveals them as signs in the outer and inner world. Every sign is imbued with the Truth, and manifests one or more of Its names and attributes, though in the ineffable Name of God they are supremely undifferentiated. This is what makes creation and speech open to the Holy Name.

The Self has entered a covenant with the self: the Self confers reality upon the self, and the self attains fullness by testifying that there is no self but the Self. When the self speaks, its only truth is in the speech of the Self. But when the self (and thus the Self) speaks, its speech can always take on form; and though bounded, it confirms the boundlessness of the Self which manifests Itself in that speech. The self, therefore, cannot attain reality without a relationship with the sacrosanct, the inviolable. Only through this relationship can it accept and understand that revelation is the way to receive Reality and return to It.

The world, humankind and the book are manifestations of the Self. There are a myriad worlds, people and books, but their essence—the "enduring debt" they owe to God for their existence—bears witness to an Ineffable Name that is one and the same. The Divine I manifests itself by speaking in and through the self. The covenant between the self and the Self opens form to distance and closeness. This act of speaking, which opens form to infinity, is summed up in the Opening.[1] It is spoken "In the name of God, the Merciful, the Compassionate."

Since speech has form and therefore duality, nothing that is opposed to mercy can be first principle. Mercy alone encompasses all, and exceeds all wrath. In the Opening, every self speaks the speech of the Self, thus transforming every place and time into a mosque. Through the Opening, the self bows down in worship with the worlds and joins in the praise of God, who has placed existence in debt to reality and righteousness. This will be manifested when the debt is returned to Him:

> Praise belongs to God, the Lord of all Being,
> the All-merciful, the All-compassionate,
> the Master of the Day of Doom.

Each individual self in the mosque of the world is called to submit willingly to God and to ask Him in the mosque for realization, for fullness of being:

> Thee only we serve: to Thee alone we pray for succour.
> Guide us in the upright path,
> the path of those whom Thou hast blessed,
> not of those against whom Thou art wrathful,
> nor of those who are astray. Amen.

The "upright path" means the path to the Self, from the names to the Named, from praise to the Praised, from the world to its Lord, from the submission to the Peace, so that the self may repay its debt, righteously and in full, by returning itself to the King who is I in and with all things. Returning one's self on the Day of Repayment brings revelation. Then our face looks into the Face, every word acquires its full meaning, and we human beings stand upright in the fairest stature. Our orientation is entirely toward Him, which also means toward ourselves. All otherness is excluded, and all names are His.

Only the upward path reveals itself as reality and bliss. The opposite is nothingness, in which wrath manifests itself as the opposite of mercy. Existence in submission means nothing if it is not gathered together into a point through which the upward path passes. And so every place and time gains something of revelation if it is connected with the Day of Repayment and the Upward Path.

Space receives and suffers us, and we receive and suffer time. We are trapped in space, and time determines for us the incessant flow of all things, of which we are and are not part. We are part of the flow, because we cannot wholly transcend our earthly captivity. And we are not part, because we are open to Oneness and to Oneness alone, which enables us to transcend the duality which binds us.

The phases and positions of Sun and Moon are signs through which we are called from our aimlessness to turn and face the Holy Mosque—so that, wherever we are, we may belong to that sign of Oneness from which everything originates and to which everything returns. This means that our will, which has the potential to follow any orientation, is called and directed to this act of recognition in space and time. By recognizing, the self becomes involved via time and space with all of existence, and its receptiveness and action is turned toward Oneness.

Thus the self confirms that it is on the path. Wherever this act of recognition and confirmation occurs, the self finds itself in one of the circles that tell of the Center, of the Truth that is in all things.

Moving toward the Center that lies outside the self enables us to draw closer to our own inner center. Although everything in the outer and the inner worlds reveals itself as duality, the path along which the signs speak of the signified leads to Oneness, and does so via knowledge of the self. When the will is tamed through submission, it is transformed into love for the Oneness that is revealed by all the multiplicity of existence.

Love for the sublime is inspired and transformed by the knowledge that the traveler has at each station, where nothing is acceptable but the Complete. Space and time are suffused and ordered by Him who is in and above all things. True love wishes only for Him, and thus even knowing the world and humankind happens for His sake.

## 12. THE DEBT

The testimony that there is no god but God and that the Praiser is His messenger comes from the will of the self, which contains the Will of the Self. These two wills are free, and hence they can be linked by trust. Since the will of the self is contingent, it can be guided and won over by aligning itself with the Will of the Self. As the Self is the only reality of the self, seeing only the Self brings liberation from fallacy and illusion.

The will of the self achieves perfection when it becomes wholly subordinate and identical to the Will of the Self. Then it is on the path to transcending the duality of will and Will.

Everything in the inner and outer worlds is beauty, or its contingent absence. There is nothing that does not manifest God's love. Sin is when human will opposes the Will of God and prevents itself from seeing the declaration of love in all things, whereas willing submission to God means discovering that everything radiates one and the same beauty.

It is worth rejecting everything, including the self as part of everything, in order to return to everything. It is worth dying in the self, for its reality lies not in the self but the Self. The center of the self lies in

God, who is both the Center and edge of everything. And submission to Him is the path that leads toward that Center.

Four ways of confirming the Testimony make up this path of submission. The first is prayer, which confirms in place and time that God is the center of all existence, and that the human heart serves this centrality. The second is the act of giving from what is lent to us as property, thus confirming that the soul is cleansed by returning everything to God via others. The third is fasting: abstaining from worldly needs, thus confirming that God is our provider, who sends down provisions and commands. And the fourth is the *hajj* to the Holy Mosque, which confirms that the inner and the outer centers are one and the same, and are wholly independent of the phenomena through which the Holy One manifests Himself.

With these expressions of submission which confirm the Testimony (prayer, cleansing through alms, fasting and pilgrimage), the self returns to its primal poverty and becomes the All-Wealthy's steward throughout existence. By owning nothing, the self gains all.

Perseverance in these aspects of submission is the pre-condition and starting-point for faith, as expressed by its six elements. The first is the Testimony, by which the will is transformed into love and knowledge. The second is understanding that the visible world is merely the manifestation of an invisible, higher reality, that this higher world of the Spirit rules the lower, and that the earth and heavens are merely signs that signify the higher world—the heavens signifying the Spirit, and the earth the soul. The third is accepting that God reveals Himself through the whole of creation and through us human beings, and that He sends down his entire revelation in books via the hearts and tongues of His messengers. The fourth is knowing that the chosen prophets and messengers—all 124,000 of them, from Adam to the Praiser—achieved self-realization by testifying how we are created in the fairest stature and in the image of the All-Merciful. The fifth is accepting that the visible world, in its individual parts and as a whole, is merely the underside of existence, but that it also manifests another World where love and death, good and evil, eternity and time, infinity and space find their only response in God's Oneness and the return of all things to that Oneness. And the sixth is knowing that the Supreme God determines both good and evil.

Once the self has cleansed itself and opened its heart to faith—that is, to love and knowledge—this act of submission reveals itself in Beauty. This means that the self serves God as if it could see Him, for though it sees Him not, He sees it.

In the phenomena of this world, where selves have lost their primal verticality and thus their link with the center which is their home, it is possible to recognize the fall and end of that existence in which we are the sum of all creation. This directs us as individuals to the need to be more resolute in associating ourselves with the Anointed One and the Praiser, so as to avoid the trials of the "last days."

And all this, as the Praiser says, is the debt of which we were told by God through the Angel Gabriel.[1] Since God has given us all that is ours, and since we have entered into a covenant of trust regarding its repayment and the final judgment on our whole relationship, the understanding and confirming of our debt to God pervades all times and spaces of human existence.

The scope of that debt is shown by the fact that we stand at the lowest point of the valley, and by our potential to recognize, in the signs of the visible world, their model in another, higher and invisible world.

But here, down in the valley, our heart is indestructible. Its sign is the Holy Mosque. If we make our heart pure, we stand upright along the axis of the worlds, the upright path, thus turning ourselves toward the Spirit, as signified by the Further Mosque. On the Night of Power, we are transported from the Holy Mosque to the Further Mosque, and from there to "the Lote-Tree of the utmost boundary."[2] At this tree, which only the Praiser or the Realised can pass, we see how Oneness manifests and gathers together all things: "With Me is all journeys' end."[3]

# 13. POVERTY

Although the heavens and the earth, like humankind itself, were created to make it known that He Is the Truth, they are all poor, utterly poor, for they give nothing to God. Whenever the self becomes fixated on the world or with itself, though both are merely signs of God, it takes these signs to be gods—that is, it associates other things with God.

Everything we have, we receive from God. Turning this fact into action means accepting that the self is in a state of total debt. The question of the self is a question asked by the giver; and the receiver returns the question to the giver. But return also confirms arrival. In love for one's parents, the self as receiver transforms itself into giver. The self's existence stems from Oneness, as manifested through one's parents. The commandment to be gentle to one's parents and to speak kindly to them confirms them as the place where Oneness is revealed; but the self must not take this place to be the Self. Hence, "speaking kindly" is a way to return to Oneness, though the self may be transcended through distance—that is, through unification by the exclusion of speech. But as the Merciful says in the Recitation: "God forgives not that aught should be with Him associated; less than that He forgives to whomsoever He will."[1]

Since God has no other, the self's duality is that of God and nothing: we can only realize ourselves in God by recognizing that all that is not God is nothing. Associating other things with God may take the most diverse forms.

The worst is to take the places and times that God has ordained as His own, and the prophets, books and forms of worship that He has revealed, to be anything other than the path that leads to Him. Only He is dependent on nothing and no-one—as He says, "God is the All-sufficient; you are the needy ones."[2]

Accepting that the Praiser is the fairest example means confirming that every subject of faith—that is, of knowledge and love—is merely a sign that praises God. "I was sent," the Praiser said, "with words that encompass everything."[3] Thus one can turn toward the Face of God through phenomena and their names, in all their fullness of meaning. Praising God as the Lord of the worlds, who instigates and reflects love, raises the Praiser from the lower to the higher Treasury of knowledge, and does so incessantly, up to and beyond the ultimate boundary.

The summit of human potential is evidenced by our piety, which is more than mere orientation in space or subjugation to time. True piety is the submission which leads to faith—that is, to love and knowledge, which are confirmed by giving.[4]

Responsibility to the needy is responsibility to God, which means to oneself. The human self has the ability to turn inward, seeing its bodily state as animal and subordinate, and hence distinct from the self which is illumined by the Spirit. In so doing, the self differentiates between sacrifice and awareness as the ultimate potential for approaching and uniting with Reality. "And the beasts of sacrifice—We have appointed them for you as among God's waymarks; there is good for you. So mention God's Name over them, standing in ranks; then, when their flanks collapse, eat of them and feed the beggar and the suppliant. So We have subjected them to you; haply you will be thankful. The flesh of them shall not reach God, neither their blood, but consciousness from you shall reach Him."[5]

By recognizing Oneness as the current of all existence and sacrificing all that is subordinate to the Self, we gain It.[6] Consciousness of and with the Self in and above all things brings oneness with His will which manifests itself in all things.

Hence, when we sacrifice, we bear witness that there is nothing in the outer and inner worlds that is without His inextinguishable Truth. The human heart thus becomes the site of unification and differentiation—that is, the Holy Mosque. All that is external to the heart is subordinate to it, for the external is merely the manifestation in differentiated form of what is gathered together in the heart.

Everything, including the sacrificed, is external to and separate from the heart, whether in its manifestation or in its return; but the purpose of everything other than Oneness is to reveal Oneness.

Turning toward the Holy Mosque, and cleansing it, is impossible without ascending from the lower toward the higher, toward the recognition and protection of human dignity: "And what shall teach thee what is the steep? The freeing of a slave, or giving food upon a day of hunger to an orphan near of kin or a needy man in misery."[7]

Taking responsibility for the needy and the weak, therefore, means drawing closer to God, as He tells humankind on the Day of Doom:

"Son of Adam, I was sick and you did not visit Me." And he will reply: "How could I visit You, when You are the Lord of the worlds?" And He will respond: "Did you not know that so-and-so My servant was sick, but you did not visit him? Did you not know that if you had visited him, you would have found Me with him?"[8]

If the path to God is contingent on respect and responsibility for the needy as other, how can the self attain its goal if poverty is not its supreme example? Is not avarice a sign that the wealthy has lost all that He has revealed from His treasury? Does He not say:

Gross rivalry diverts you,
even till you visit the tombs.
No indeed; but soon you shall know.[9]

Our original state is one of poverty. In acknowledging this, the first man had everything: all of Paradise was his. This made him the image of his Lord: in the fullness of poverty, he was open to the fullness of the Lord. The forbidden tree and his heart, as a duality bridged by memory, served only to confirm Oneness.

All the signs in the outer and inner worlds clearly revealed the Lord to His servant. But when he reached for the forbidden fruit in order to possess it, he lost his poverty, and with it his openness to the Complete. To return to the Complete, we need to recognize and accept our primal poverty. Then we shall have worlds with which to praise God, instead of worldly goods which seem to praise us. To be poor does not mean having little: it means having God, and thus having all that reveals Him.

## 14. MARY

The innermost part of every mosque is its *mihrab*—the niche in the wall that faces toward Mecca. Every mosque has at least one door through which it may be entered physically; but the *mihrab* can be described as the door which all the signs within the mosque speak of, and which all its paths lead toward. Before that door, the door to the inviolable sanctuary, we complete our immersion in the holy teachings and sacred rituals, our struggle with the duality that we must transform into Oneness by the testimony that there is no self but the Self. Here we seek, expecting to find everything. We knock on the door, hoping that it will open. This is the place where we call and where we are silent, awaiting the response from the One who hears and sees all.

We enter the mosque from the world and society, in order to confirm our dignity in its deepest sense—as the center through which we gather together all of existence and return it to Oneness.

The *mihrab* denotes the human heart or the pure soul. Many of the world's *mihrabs* are inscribed with the phrase: "Whenever Zachariah entered the *mihrab*." This is part of the verse in the Recitation which reads in full:

> Whenever
> Zachariah went in to her
> in the mihrab, he
> found her provisioned.
> "Mary," he said,
> "how comes this to thee?"
> "From God," she said.
> Truly God provisions
> whomsoever He will
> without reckoning.[1]

The priest Zachariah enters the *mihrab* where the Virgin Mary is. The *mihrab* is the center of the mosque: all worship faces it and issues from it. It is like the mosque's main door, through which one passes from the lower to the higher world, from the body to the Spirit, or like the door through which one passes into the world and the body.

The Virgin tells the righteous old priest that all provisions come from God. This is the mystery of all existence, and of humankind's place within it. Through the Virgin's conviction that God provides all, together with her submission and purity, she receives the supreme gift—the Holy Spirit, that manifests itself in and through her as the Word.[2]

By dwelling in the *mihrab*, she dwelt beside the Holy Mosque. This was the supreme submission, through which she was carried to the Further Mosque, the Ultimate Boundary, the Source.

In saying that all provisions are from God, Mary confirms her testimony to Oneness. She is defined by the testimony that there is no god but God and that, as a result, praising Him is humanity's supreme potential. For her, the Holy Mosque, as the center of the outward world, is the image of the human heart. This is the duality that manifests and confirms Oneness, and Mary's testimony of it is what makes her chosen.

Since God is the All-provider, poverty is human nature. Indelibly inscribed in this is the response to God's question: "Am I not your Lord? Mary guarded her virginity, so We breathed into her of Our Spirit, and she confirmed the Words of her Lord and His Books, and became one of the obedient."[3]

As the Lord in the Recitation says: "And when the angels said, 'Mary, God has chosen thee, and purified thee; He has chosen thee above all women. Mary, be obedient to thy Lord, prostrating and bowing before Him.'"[4] And the angels went on to say: "Mary, God gives thee good tidings of a Word from Him whose name is Messiah, Jesus, son of Mary; high honoured shall he be in this world and the next, near stationed to God."[5]

Our fairest stature enables us to enjoy the fruits of the heights: therefore we are in both the depths of the waters and the heights of heaven. Beside Mary's uprightness, which receives the Spirit and gives the Word, there is a palm tree. When she was seized in that lonely place by the pangs of childbirth, a voice spoke to her: "Nay, do not sorrow; see, thy Lord has set below thee a rivulet. Shake also to thee the palm-trunk, and there shall come tumbling upon thee dates fresh and ripe. Eat therefore, and drink, and be comforted."[6]

This voice calling to Mary to remember her uprightness from water to the Spirit, her pure humanity that links the earth and the heavens, finds its echo in the Praiser's words about the palm tree, "which resembles the submissive one who, with the permission of his Lord, gives fruits at all seasons and whose leaves do not fall."[7]

In her submission beside the Holy Mosque, between water and the Spirit, mercy manifests itself in Mary's womb—as the Word. The Word and the fruit of her womb unite the *mihrab* with the source, uniting earthly presence with the Flow through which Oneness manifests Itself:

> And We made Mary's son, and his mother,
> to be a sign, and gave them refuge
> upon a height, where was a hollow
> and a spring.[8]

Jesus the Messiah, son of Mary, is received and accepted as the Word of God. He too bore witness that only in humility and poverty may human nature receive the baptism of our Lord. In his utter humility and poverty, he made his heart into a Pure House of God, in which it was revealed that there is no self but the Self. In his knowledge and

being he testified to the Truth of the All-merciful from Whom all provisions come, praying before his disciples:

> "O God, our Lord, send
> down upon us a Table
> out of heaven, that shall
> be for us a festival, the
> first and last of us,
> and a sign from Thee.
> And provide for us: Thou
> art the best of providers."
> God said, "Verily I
> do send it down on you;
> whoso of you hereafter
> disbelieves, verily I
> shall chastise him with a
> chastisement wherewith I
> chastise no other being."[9]

# 15. "PURIFY MY HOUSE"

One of the Messenger traditions relates that the first mosque to be built on this earth was the one in the Bekka valley, which God sent down as a sign of His covenant with Adam, when Adam was banished from Eden and began his earthly life.[1] The second was the mosque on the Holy Mount, the Further Mosque, erected forty years after the first.[2]

Both were built in accordance with God's will and humanity's submission to it. Before the Fall, all the worlds were humanity's mosque; everything in them was as God ordained when He bestowed them on humankind. This relationship between God as Lord and humankind as servant was signified by the central place of the inviolable in the world and the human heart. These were identical—the forbidden tree or the Holy Mosque,[3] and the inviolable center or the human heart, two houses open only to God.

But since God creates all things anew at every moment in time, it is forbidden to accept any image before Him. God's "I am" means that all other gods are forbidden to us. Making gods means incising or engraving images of anything in heaven, on earth or in the waters; and praying to or serving them is also forbidden. Whenever a person turns to God, one image is destroyed and another accepted. But no image can be allowed to take the place of God, even for an instant.

Since no image can be God, cleansing the heart of that image, acknowledging that the heart is forbidden to all but Him, means turning toward God. Full submission to Him is freedom; in it the inviolable heart finds reality, for all things perish except His Face.

When humankind disobeyed the ban on approaching the outward center, the inviolable nature of inner and outer was riven apart into the signs in the outer world and the signs in the selves. Our turning toward God prompts us to renew the covenant written at the core of our being by saying "Yes" to God's question "Am I not your Lord?" Keeping that covenant entails submission to God's will in orientation, thought, and deed.

The covenant, therefore, requires one to accept God's commandment to make and keep pure the center of the world, thus ensuring pureness of heart and oneness in multiplicity. This opens the way for us to recall and reaffirm that all things come from God, and not to recognize any god but God in anything—neither in our selves, nor in worldly phenomena, nor in our handiwork.

In that covenant, however, there remains the possibility that we may forget, or turn toward non-Self. Our will can accept and implement, or can reject and disobey. For both mosques, there have been times when human souls were made pure and when they were benighted, and their condition reflects this state of purity or darkness.

In Abraham's day, both temples were in ruins. In the Recitation, God speaks of the purification and building of the First Mosque:

> And when We settled for Abraham the place
> of the House: "Thou shall not associate
> with Me anything. And do thou purify
> My House for those that shall go about it
> and those that stand, for those that bow
> and prostrate themselves,
> and proclaim among men the Pilgrimage."[4]

The purification of the Holy Mosque means returning it to its original purpose: that of bearing witness to Oneness as the source and destination of all existence. Recognizing and acknowledging that the

Holy Mosque is a sign of return is a consequence of purifying the human heart, since there is no peace but Peace.

Restoring the self's primal nature means renewing its link with primal Peace. Whenever the heart loses direct contact with the Spirit, it becomes benighted, defiled and frustrated; and when human individuals reach this state, they introduce gods other than God into the Holy Mosque and the Further Mosque. The human heart becomes obsessed with these gods, and with the violence and destruction that are the inevitable consequence.

As humans, we are at constant risk of forgetting; and whenever we forget, human purposes in thought and deed—worldly phenomena, in other words—become our gods. We forget that all things come from God and that there is no god but Him. Conversely, attempts at renewal have meant escaping from gods into God, from illusion into Reality. Here our example has been set by the prophets—Adam, Noah, Abraham, Jesus, and a long succession of others. For all of them, the center of the world, which corresponds to the heart, became their refuge, for it was in and through this center that they turned to the Face.

Time and again, from Adam to Abraham, the Holy Mosque and the Further Mosque suffered defilement and destruction, followed by purification and rebuilding. Abraham purified and rebuilt them, becoming their warden through his testament, and the guarantor of humanity's covenant with God through his prayer:

> Our Lord, receive this from us; Thou art
>     the All-hearing, the All-knowing;
> and, our Lord, make us submissive to Thee,
> and of our seed a nation submissive
> to Thee; and show us our holy rites, and
> turn towards us; surely Thou turnest,
>     and art All-compassionate;
> and, our Lord, do Thou send among them
> a Messenger, one of them, who shall recite
> to them Thy signs, and teach them the Book
> and the wisdom, and purify them; Thou art
>     the All-mighty, the All-wise.[5]

Abraham paid his debt in full[6], and he is therefore a good example for whoever hopes for God and the Last Day.[7] A sign of this is his purification of the Holy Houses. After Abraham the Mosques again endured times of desecration and destruction, followed by purification and rebuilding. These times reflect how we first forgot and then remembered what was bestowed on us, as God in the Recitation tells.[8]

When gods other than God were taken, when people relied on a warden other than Him and unrest spread through the earth, both Mosques were turned into houses of merchandise and then destroyed.[9] The unshakable center of the human self, however, found itself once again; and when God was remembered and His Name called out, this led to the purification and restoration of the mosque.

Neither our deepest center nor the place that God had ordained could be destroyed. Returning to ourselves also means returning to the pure mosque: though external place and the human heart are a duality in the realm of existence, they are one in the Treasury.

When the Prophet went out into the world, the First Mosque was surrounded by statues and the rites associated with them, and the Second Mosque was buried under piles of rubbish. Then he called for all gods to be denied but God. He called for the interdiction to be acknowledged so that the heart could confirm its purification through the purification of both mosques: the Holy Mosque in the Valley and the Further Mosque on the Mount.

In so doing, he accepted the Virgin's testimony that all things are from God, and joined in her son's prayer that God should provide for the people by sending down a table from heaven, in other words, that they should know the reality behind phenomena.

When the Praiser traveled by night from the Holy Mosque to the Further Mosque, the circle of descent and ascent was closed. The visible world was shown to be the extension and manifestation of the Invisible. What began with the Intellect and Spirit before differentiation was fulfilled in the purity of the Praiser's heart:

> My heart was extracted and it was washed with the water of Zamzam and then it was restored in its original position, after which it was filled with faith and wisdom.[10]

# 16. The Ascension

Human dignity is inseparable from free will, which comprises all potential, from self-realization to the furthest bounds of non-reality. This means that only the self can choose to face the Self or the non-Self. Everything else in existence chooses the Self by its very nature.

The human heart is sensitive not only to all these changes, but also to the distinction between the Real and the non-real. Yet the fact that humanity is subject to the duality of all that exists means that we are caught between remembering and forgetting, between knowledge and ignorance.

The Real lies in the very path of those who orient themselves toward it. But Reality possesses all that exists; and nothing that exists possesses Reality. We are wholly dependent on it, but it depends on nothing.

Our ability to call out to the All-merciful includes His response to us. God asks us to "Turn thy face towards the Holy Mosque; and wherever you are, turn your faces towards it."[1] Though its time and place constantly changes, the heart knows the flux of all things: hence, wherever we are, we are in a mosque: "The whole earth has been made a mosque for us," the Praiser says,[2] and the human center looks toward the outward center. The human center is pure only if it acts for God and for all people.

The human self is solitude. If the self repudiates suffering and death, if it refuses to submit to the Self and opposes His Will with its own, it remains excluded from the oneness of all that is God. But if it concentrates on the Holy Mosque, which receives every orientation at its center, the self becomes purified and empty of all save the Self.

When the self draws close to the Holy Mosque, it becomes inner purity and openness to Oneness: "All things perish, except His Face."[3] This is because "He is God, One."[4] His Oneness is Unity—and the human heart is open to that Oneness, is its pure image. By turning toward the Holy Mosque, the pure heart confirms that it chooses nothing but the Self, and the self that it realizes itself in remembering, in turning toward God.

God tells in the Recitation how the Praiser journeyed in a single night from the Holy Mosque in Mecca to the Further Mosque in Jerusalem. But each of us is always in the mosque of our heart, whether our soul be pure or benighted. Hence our mosque is the Holy Mosque, and every other mosque the Further Mosque; and when our soul subordinates itself wholly to the Spirit, we pass from the Holy to the Further Mosque, joining them together in the oneness of our heart. Our heart then becomes wholly illumined with the Holy Spirit, and we hear how all the signs in the outer and inner worlds praise God's Name.

All the mosques in this world, seen from the perspective of the individual self, are like the Holy and the Further Mosque. They can be linked only through their heavenly counterparts, described in the Recitation as the Lote Tree of the Utmost Boundary[5] and the House Inhabited.[6] Both names testify to God's throne, to God as first and last, inner and outer.

With the Night Journey and his Ascension, the Messenger showed how all the temples are united in praise of God's Name:

> Had God not driven back
> the people, some by the means of others,
> there had been destroyed cloisters and churches,
> oratories and mosques, wherein God's Name
> is much mentioned.[7]

People's responses to one another are a conversation in which every utterance is translatable from the language of the speaker into the language of the listener. This translatability is made possible by the Common Word, around which all human diversity has the potential to gather. This Word is the expression of God's love to be known. The Common Word remains hidden, even when uncovered, but it may be called through His myriad names, each of which proclaims and confirms it:

> Say: "People of the Book! Come now to a word
> common between us and you, that we serve
> none but God, and that we associate not
> aught with Him, and do not some of us take
> others as Lords, apart from God."[8]

This Common Word is one and the same in every language, although it takes different forms. Though every form points to it, none can ever wholly reveal it, because it is the ineffable Name of God, to which all the different doctrines and rites are linked. This Name is at the center of every doctrine and rite, and at the same time is one with the single unchanging human heart that lies "between God's two fingers."

Monasteries, churches, synagogues, and mosques are alive only with Him and the mention of Him—without Him, they are defunct. Different teachings and forms of worship, therefore, are gathered around this Word that is one and the same. In monasteries, churches, synagogues, and mosques, the debt to the Common Word gives rise to will (awe), faith (love and knowledge) and virtue (saintliness).[9] Both the Word and the Name gather together all that is differentiated.

The language and meaning of the monasteries are abstracted from phenomena so that they may be more clearly seen through and with the Name of God. As for the Holy Mosque, humanity needs to accept that it shows how we are inseparable from our human center and that our inner openness to Oneness cannot be destroyed. Only then can the Further Mosque, which is the symbol of the manifestation and descent of Oneness into phenomena from the first Intellect to the human heart, be revealed as the countless multitude of Names and the voice that calls them.

In the human heart, the whole world becomes a mosque. The Names of Him who is revealed by the world are called in a myriad of voices, which come from the one Mystery and forever return toward it.

## 17. THE HOLY

God says: "*Alif Lam Mim*. That is the Book, wherein is no doubt, a guidance to the conscious who believe in the Unseen."[1] The three characters that begin this statement reveal the oneness of the word that is confirmed by a countless multitude of manifestations—the world and humankind as a book with two aspects. The first is differentiated and scattered through the outer world. The second is gathered together within us as humans. But both are the one same face of the Divine I. As this I speaks in all things, It descends into the deepest center and manifests Itself as the third book.

The Mystery is thus both present in duality and constantly transcending it. All the signs in the outer and inner worlds lead through it, but never into it. The highest potential of the led is to be led toward the Mystery. The led believe in the Mystery; and this means that what we know through the two books—the book of the world and the book of humankind—and their summing up in the book that is spoken, heard, and written, can never be perfect knowledge. As a result, in and beyond all such knowledge lies love, the need to be wholly satisfied; and nothing satisfies the self but the Self.

The Self is both infinitely distant and infinitely near. All knowledge includes love, and all love includes knowledge. Hence the self is what it knows, but the self loves what is designated by that knowledge, and hence it is what it loves. But since nothing in the outer and inner worlds, none of the scattered and reassembled signs, can satisfy the self, it constantly reaches beyond what it has attained, constantly moving toward the Loved that it cannot attain. In everything it experiences it feels a sense of lack, for the duality in which it lives is evidence that Oneness is never the same as its manifestations in the countless multitude of phenomena.

When God says that He is hidden and loves to be known, and that this is why He creates, He does not say that He changes. He is One and the Same, First and Last, Outer and Inner. Hence He is always hidden, but His love to be known, and thus to be understood, never ceases.

When we see creation, differentiation makes knowledge possible. But the signified is always greater than the knower: this is why it is the Loved. Neither the knower nor the lover may attain the Known and Loved, for the latter is the Holy. This is why all joy and satisfaction is tinged with sadness.

Although all signs lead to the Loved, although He is the only reality, He cannot be seen, even though all the signs in outer and inner worlds speak of Him. He cannot be reached through the senses, but remains in the night of faith, in the heart of the submissive servant who perseveres on his journey. The signs speak of Him, for without Him they are without light or voice. This is the Mystery of all the signs and all the voices that descend from the Mystery and ascend to it again.

We who are guided desire the clear voice of our guide, but it cannot be heard through the senses, for the guide is deep and exalted, mysterious and concealed, and speaks in the deepest aspirations of the self. The guide is the voice in the night by which the Self calls to Itself through the self and all that is in the outer world.

The call of the Loved in all the inner and outer worlds is their whole existence. He is not merely speech: He is all, and what touches the skin, what reaches the ears and eyes, the nose and mouth, merely denotes Him. He does not just call to people with His voice, but with the whole of existence, with every event and every circumstance. He is not surface, and therefore not obvious: hence the self is called upon not merely to live on the surface, but to see in speech the manifestation of Oneness. His call is deep, for it is utterly near. His call is hidden; and with it He guides the self toward the Complete.

When the self hears the call, it embarks on the journey, but never arrives. It discovers the closeness of the Self, but also its own evergreater distance from the Self. Knowing the Self means constantly seeking It. The call of the Self is incessant and unknown.

No self can say that it cannot be heard from anywhere, nor that there is any point toward which one should finally face. The call demands that one constantly travel and turn toward Him. The self changes unceasingly by means of this, shedding all that is not the Self. So too change all signs on the horizon and within the self. Within its own forms, speech is able to receive these changes.

The caller always calls with His creation and His love. The call is like the song of a bird in the night, on the hills or in the desert: the beauty of each song is one and the same, whether it comes from here or there, from close or far away. The response is to set off in quest of beauty, but beauty speaks only of the Hidden One.

The journey has no other goal but the house in which everything is with the Self. In other words, to arrive at the Holy Mosque, the pure heart in which the Host and His guest are one and the same—the Complete that manifests itself in the countless multitude of signs.

## 18. THE NAME

The more we become accustomed to the space that receives us, the more it presents to us the side that faces non-Self, nothingness. Habit leads us to believe that the place where we are is at the top of the ladder by which we climbed to it—that we are at the summit, the end of the ascent.

But the Face of God is everywhere, and He responds to the call of humankind. Nothing can surpass that Face. As we draw near to Him, passing from the self as reality through the various levels of His manifestation, all illusion evaporates.

Liberation from the habit of seeing the surface of signs enables us to remember that we are guests, and that nothing in the inner or outer worlds is ours. The Name of God is revealed to us in all the breadth of the earth, all the heights of the heavens and all that lies between. In the light of His Name, everything before us becomes recognized as a table spread from God. We are travelers on the path to Oneness, and all phenomena in the inner and outer worlds are only signs along that path. They too are all gathered within the Name.

This is why Noah left the expanses of earth and surrendered his soul to the Spirit on the face of the waters, surrendered his fate to the Will that steered the ark across the expanses of the ocean.

This is why Abraham left his home and his city, and set off into the open desert that reached farther than the eye could see, to renew his memory of the Ruler and Provider by seeing the same Oneness in the outer world and his own inner center—all for love of the One Who had announced His Name to him.

The same reason prompted Moses to abandon the luxury of Egypt and guided him along the desert and mountain paths.

With the same dedication to his own inner center, Jesus knew that the mercy of the One Who manifests Himself in creation transcends and suffuses all the signs in all their states.

These and all other prophets denied that the world had any cause other than the Creator. Their journeys were the realization of the testimony that there is no god but God and that the Praiser is His servant and messenger. The Name of God is the only true wealth we have at any place and time; and so the reality of all things lies in our existing in the Name of God and in praising Him through our testimony.

The I that is the hidden Treasure is also the Mystery. Proclaiming the Mystery turns the hidden Name into presence: when our human selves call the Self by His Name, God reveals Himself. Every phenomenon has its own name in the Hidden Treasury; and when it becomes existent, its names are revealed. We encompass all that is in existence by knowing all the names that God taught us.[1]

All these names, which God has taught us, enable us to see everything in the outer and inner worlds as provisions from God, as the treasury that He sends down. In their entirety, these names grant us the ability to call to God. Our knowledge of all the names includes those which we may use to summon Him, as well as the names of all the phenomena that manifest the various attributes of the Named. Calling to God by His Name is humanity's supreme potential:

> Say: "Call upon God, or call upon
> the Merciful; whichsoever you call
> upon, to Him belong the Names
> Most Beautiful."[2]

It is through His most beautiful names that the whole of existence—the earth, the heavens, and all that lies between—proclaims the Ineffable Name, the Treasury where God has His being. In telling of Him, all the differentiated signs in the outer world manifest the Name that is one and the same through all the myriad phenomena. What is sent down into existence speaks His Name, and cleaves to it in the tiniest individuality and in all the created worlds.

The potential of the human heart to gather together and unite all this differentiation also includes the potential to receive the Ineffable Name which manifests itself in the most beautiful names. By calling out the various names in a myriad of places and times, we orient ourselves toward the Sublime who manifests Himself in descent and ascent:

> He knows what penetrates into the earth,
>> and what comes forth from it,
> what comes down from heaven, and what goes up unto it.
> He is with you wherever you are; and God sees
>> the things you do.[3]

God is immanent in His Name, which is sacrosanct, inviolable, separate from every presence but His. By calling out His Name, we turn toward the knowledge of all things. Through His Name, we become the site where all of existence becomes manifest. He is the ultimate achievement of every act of descent, but also the potential for full return and ascent, for He knows all the names. Indeed, ascent takes place through the names:

> A questioner asked of a chastisement about to fall
>> for the unbelievers, which none may avert,
>> from God, the Lord of the Stairways.
> To Him the angels and the Spirit mount up in a day
>> whereof the measure is fifty thousand years.[4]

All spaces and all times exist in God's Name. By calling out His Name, the self submits to Him in the valley of existence. In so doing, it elevates itself to the primacy which is total otherness, and to the outermost which is the innermost.

In accepting that God has being in His Name, which proclaims and unites the whole of creation, as callers we renew the heavenly sacrifice which is included in creation. In so doing, we transform the descent through the macrocosm into an ascent through the microcosm, gathering together all our being and entering as a unity into the all-encompassing Name of God, into the undifferentiated and primal Oneness of the supreme Principle whose essence is identical to the Name.

The secret encounter of created and Uncreated, contingent and Complete, finite and Infinite, temporal and Eternal, takes place in the Name of God.

The Name that manifests God includes His presence, which becomes so active that the Name possesses the self that calls it. In focusing on the sign of infinity, we attain infinity itself:

> For when the individual subject becomes identified with the Name to the point where all mental projection is absorbed by the form of the Name, then its Divine Essence manifests spontaneously, since this sacred form tends toward nothing outside of itself. It has a positive affinity with its Essence alone, wherein its limits finally dissolve. Thus it is that union with the Divine Name becomes Union with God Himself.[5]

# 19. THE PEACE

When we accept the call to turn our face toward the Holy Mosque in the sacred Vale of Tears,[1] we become a point on the circle formed by all the potential responders to that call. All these responders face the Center that is one and the same. Their hearts—that is, the centers of all these selves—constitute, together with the one Center which they face, a confirmation of oneness in multiplicity and multiplicity in oneness.

The Center is the principle of all that lies outside it. It irradiates all with its fullness, and reveals itself through a countless multitude of circles and phenomena, each of which manifests harmony and order as its link with the principle, with the peace, beauty, and justice of the Center.

Every self displays a duality—the outward Center that is one and the same for all, and the inner center that is its own. When one concentrates on oneness in both inner and outer worlds, beauty shows itself as the light of Truth, the manifestation of Peace and the call to Peace. In everything that manifests itself as beauty, there is also a sign and manifestation of the Name.

If the Center is infinitely distant, it is the One; but as the Complete, it is also infinitely near. Hence the outward and the inward center are one and the same. This means that there is no center but the Center, for only God can be the Center of all things. When the self faces this Center, God is in this orientation, but it is not God.[2]

As long as the self faces God, it is on the periphery; but its goal is to dissolve the peripheral and to find itself at the center, in the pure heart which is the house of God, the abode of Peace.[3] Taking this as its starting-point, therefore, the self moves toward the Holy Mosque, or Oneness; and in so doing becomes ever more the servant of the Lord, His steward on earth.

The self draws ever closer to the Self, and its innermost center becomes the pure image of the Face, yearning for knowledge and love, beauty and justice as the expressions of Peace. All this is possible only for a self that has excluded every presence other than His. This is why His Name is constantly spoken: so that It may receive in Itself the whole of being.

Even when we orient ourselves away from our own center and toward the outer center, away from the self and toward the world, we are still turning toward ourselves, for we are the total of everything in the outer world. Transcending duality means realizing the self in the Self, the center in the Center. It means finding an answer to the outward differentiation between earth and heaven and the inner differentiation between soul and Spirit. The soul purifies itself, submits and surrenders to the Spirit, and thus returns to its Lord in peace, well-pleased and well pleasing.[4]

Finding peace in itself, the soul recognizes peace in the outer world, in others who are also oriented toward the same Holy Mosque. In turning their faces to the right and left, those who pray in the universal Mosque of the world broadcast the peace they have received from the Name, along with their self-realization in Him. God is peace. Peace lies at every human's very center, in its pre-eternal oath. Only through peace at one's center can one know and uphold that peace on earth in which all that is beautiful reveals and upholds Peace.

Submission to God means holding to peace as the center of all things. To submit means to acquiesce. Acquiescence is the relationship between the human being who grows quiet in God, and God as the Peace that quietens. And yearning for peace is the same as yearning for God. At the core of our being, we humans holds the memory of the peace that gained experience of bearing witness to God's overlordship before our Fall into the world of forgetting. Only by being aware of this debt, and accepting how it must be repaid, can the self return to the place and time of peace—to the reality of Eden, that is, to God's presence. "God guides whosoever follows His good pleasure in the ways of peace, and brings them forth from the shadows into the light by His leave; and He guides them to a upright path."[5]

And submission is one's relationship with the Peace. Only by accepting this can one come to know the sanctity of the Center and its openness to peace in motion, to motion in peace.

The Holy Mosque is the human heart. If its sign is the outward center toward which all people can turn, all must have their own appropriate place and time for their primal purpose—that is, the link with the Principle. This makes it possible to establish an equilibrium between dualities, thus clearly manifesting the oneness they confirm.

In facing the Center, we affirm our place in the Vale of Tears, where we came when all potential descended and became manifest. Here we are at the lowest ebb of our potential, at the furthest limit of being, which brushes against non-being. Melancholia and sadness pervade us. At this level of existence, in our sadness and disorientation, we receive the word: "When the signs of the All-merciful were recited to them, they fell down prostrate, weeping."[6]

In this darkness, this Vale of Tears, we find ourselves in the Name that reveals Itself to us; and in this Name we find our ancestral peace, the call to take the upright path that leads us away from non-Self. By finding itself in the Name, the self arrives at the Further Mosque and experiences how all of existence manifests the descent of the Spirit into the night.

Only by knowing how far one can descend into non-Self can we sense our destiny, which is one of beauty and justice. Whatever the darkness or oblivion experienced by the self, there is always a ray of the Self which is light, which turns destiny away from the depths and toward the Highest. This is phrased as the Command:

> The Night of Power is better than a thousand months;
>> in it the angels and the Spirit descend,
> by the leave of their Lord, upon every command.[7]

When the presence of God's Name is made real in the heart, it becomes the center of every outward mosque. The Further Mosque is the sum of all the places in which the Name of God is mentioned. With peace in heaven, there can be peace on earth, and peace within the human self is the crux of this relationship.

Thus, from the purified Holy Mosque—that is, the purified heart—all the monasteries, churches, synagogues and mosques may be seen as the multiplicity that confirms the inner center. Only this center can grant and maintain peace in all this multiplicity, and thus transform it into the harmonious and unending praise of the One.

# Afterword

The mosque is a place where we meet the Supreme Being by expressing our submission and that of the world to Him. This submission, however, involves not only love and knowledge of the Supreme, but also a connection with the world as a whole. The mosque may be any place in all of existence.

The mosque is our relationship with God; and since that relationship is based on trust, it can take many possible directions. In the incessant flux and reflux of the world, the mosque is where we grasp our highest potential. The whole of existence is a mosque, because we humans gather together all that is manifested and differentiated throughout the worlds.

All phenomena, separately and together, have a face in time that is turned toward the Face of Eternity. All of existence vanishes before His Face, which means that all things prostrate themselves before Him, and the reality of every face lies in its reflection of the Face. The face that reflects and the Face that is reflected attest to Oneness, and thus reveal themselves to one another in their separateness and unity.

Standing before the Face, the face surrenders to it in utter humility by casting itself to the ground, thus confirming its desire for unity, to be what the Face knows. The oneness of this dual gaze unites the submission of the heart with the heart of submission. And the Face is omnipresent: wherever the face turns, it sees only the Face. Only thus may Oneness be heard, seen and spoken.

Eternal wisdom blazes at the center of each of God's prophets. This wisdom can reveal the meaning of diversity and the harmony within it. It is both eternal concealment and constant revelation. Our human center cannot be exhausted of this wisdom, and thus we can never be wholly lost.

If debt is our link with God, since we can have nothing other than what we have received, the heart of this debt is the debt of the heart—and the heart is the Throne of the Merciful, the Compassionate. Oneness manifests itself through submission to Oneness, through love and knowledge of Oneness.

Our relationship with God is one of debt; and the debt is total. This debt makes us into both receiver and giver. In receiving from God and repaying Him, we enter into a conversation, becoming a listener who receives the Word and a speaker whose words merge into the Voice, leaving no enduring image. In entering into this conversation we recognize that our life is entirely received, and that our direction is determined by our Giver. Nothing in this conversation can be abridged, for there is nothing in or with us that has not been received.

Our primal perfection demands a perfect goal: and this is none other than the call to God by the whole of creation, as the Voice commands:

> Say:"My prayer, my ritual sacrifice,
> my living, my dying—all belongs to God,
>    the Lord of all Being.
> No associate has He. Even so I have been
> commanded, and I am the first of those
>    that submit."
>
> (Qur'an, 6:162–63)

For people to achieve self-realization in this way—through an ancestral nature that is one and the same, and with an individual responsibility to a God who is one and the same—depends on submission:

on bringing our will as created beings into compliance with the Will of God as Creator. This act of coordination transcends all boundaries and rejects all gods but God.

Self-realization is the potential of every individual, for it is guaranteed by the same underlying human nature. Our ancestral nature is contingent on nothing but God. Once this fact is recognized, the self-realization of any individual includes all other individuals and peoples in the world. Our being "in" a mosque, and our "being" a mosque, expresses this potential—the potential to turn toward God, and away from every image and representation of God, at any stage on our journey. As the chosen, we can only measure and retain our presence in the mosque through righteousness. We may acknowledge or deny the fact that we are chosen, fulfil it or rebel against it, submit to it or evade it, depart from it or return to it. But however much we try, we can never reject our chosenness. Hence righteousness remains the irrefutable and indestructible content of our being.

In our quest for the paths of righteousness, we converse with God, and even ask Him about the evil and injustice that are sent to test us. But if we accept anything other than Him as justice and righteousness, we sense that we are destroying the mosque of the world, and in so doing are destroying ourselves.

> The mosques belong to God;
> so call not, along with God,
> upon anyone.

> (Qur'an, 72:18)

# Notes

William C. Chittick is professor in the Department of Comparative Studies at the State University of New York, Stony Brook. He is a leading and greatly respected scholar in the field of the classical Muslim intellectual tradition. He has published numerous books, among which are: *Imaginal Worlds: Ibn al-'Arabi and the Problem of Religious Diversity; The Sufi Path of Knowledge: Ibn al-'Arabi's Metaphysics of Imagination; The Sufi Path of Love: The Spiritual Teachings of Rumi; The Self-Disclosure of God: Principles of Ibn al-'Arabi's Cosmology; Sufism: A Short Introduction; The Heart of Islamic Philosophy: The Quest for the Self-Knowledge in the Teachings of Afdal al-Din Kāshāni.*

1. *al-Futûhât al-makkiyya* (Cairo, 1911), 2:414; cited in Chittick, *The Sufi Path of Knowledge* (Albany: SUNY Press, 1989), 171.

1. The English word "inviolable" is used in the sense of the Arabic word *harām*, which also carries the connotation of "forbidden," "sacrosanct," or "holy." This word signifies the space that is "chosen," "separated," "consecrated," and "made inviolable." It was declared as such by God, and He invites humankind to accept as forbidden any behaviour in opposition to the prescribed. The word *harām* derives from the verbal root *h-r-m*. In legal usage, the word signifies that which is excluded from prescribed behaviors and therefore punishable. Some derivations from this root carry the meanings of "inadmissibility" and "barring from," which can be

found in Recitation. *Harām* ("the forbidden") is the opposite of *halāl* ("the permitted").

It is relevant here that the Slav noun *zabrana* ("prohibition, interdiction, ban") derives from the verb *boriti se* ("to fight," "to struggle").

CHAPTER 1: THE SELF AND THE SELF

1. The corresponding translation to the Arabic name *Muhammad* should be "The Praiser." In Recitation, the name in this form is mentioned four times (3:144, 33:40, 47:2 and 48:29), and once as *Ahmad* (61:6). It should immediately be pointed out that the literal translation of this Arabic name is "The Praised" ("Praise-worthy") rather than "The Praiser." The Arabic name *Ahmad* corresponds to the translation "The Most Praised." This difference between the literal translation in passive form and the active form used here should be explained in order to avoid misunderstanding the meaning this book is directed to. According to the words of God in Recitation, *Muhammad* is "The light-giving lamp" (33:46), "A good example" (33:21), and "A mighty morality" (68:4). That he is The light-giving lamp means that, in his relationship with God as the Light (24:35) he is the recipient and, as such, lighted. Thus, God's name, Light, is realized in him. God is the Light and therefore both Lighted and Light-giving. Accordingly, *Muhammad* is the Lighted as the recipient of the Light-giving's Light. Simultaneously, he is also Light-giving with this Light he has received. However, none of the Light he is giving is his own, since there is no light but Light. The Light-giving, Light and Lighted are One. Applying the testimony that there is no god but God, it is possible to say that the Known, Knowledge and Knowing are also One, since there is no knowledge but Knowledge. The one that is Known transmits Knowledge and is therefore both the Knowing and Knowledge-giving. This corresponds to God's commandment: "Say: The knowledge is with God!"(67–26) God also commands *Muhammad* to say: "My Lord embraces all things in His knowledge!" (6:80, see also 7:89) The highest and only goal of a human being is to know God. However, reaching this goal is not possible without being. If a human being cognizes God as the Known, this means that he/she receives the Knowledge into himself/herself and that, as the cognizer, he/she is simultaneously known to the Knowing. Thus, to know oneself is to know one's Lord. With this knowledge the human being finds, inside him/herself, the Known, who is there as his/her essence. *Muhammad* is a good example exactly because his morality is the expression of the realization of God's names in him. And one of these names is *al-Hamīd/Hamīd*, which corresponds to the translation "The Praised"(see, e.g., 2:267; 11:73; 14:1; 14:8; 22:24, 64; 31:12; 34:6; 35:15; 41:42; 42:28; 57:24; 60:6; 85:8). Since the entirety of creation is giving knowledge of God's names and praises God, creation is therefore Praised, since it receives the Praise into itself. But it is

the Praiser at the same time, since it receives and radiates the fullness of Praise. The link between what is praised and The One Who made it as such is the Praise. And "Praise belongs to God!" (1:2). Thus, God is both the Praiser and the Praised. The realization of such being in *Muhammad* means that he is the Praised as Praise recipient and, therefore, the realizer of God's name The Praiser. At the same time, *Muhammad* also gives knowledge of the Praise, the receiving of which makes him the Praised and the Praiser as well. The relationship between *Muhammad* and God is the Praise. When *Muhammad* receives the Praise, he is the Praised and God is the Praiser. And when he radiates what he has received as the Lamp and Example, he is the Praiser and God is the Praised. If the testimony of Oneness is applied to these considerations as well, it is possible to say that the Praised, Praise, and Praiser, or the Praiser, Praise, and Praised are One, since there is no praised but the Praised, nor praiser but the Praiser, nor praise but the Praise. To recognize the truth of each phenomenon in the sense that there is nothing which has not been created with it (15:85) means, among other things, that Praise is in every phenomenon, and that its realization implies reaching a laudable station (17:79). From this point, the received is being returned to its source, and the Oneness is being testified there.

2. See 23:71. The majority of quotations from the Recitation (ar. *Qur'an*) in this essay are taken from the English version by Arthur J. Arberry, *The Koran Interpreted.* The use of the term "Recitation" is a translation of ar. *Qur'an.* The reasons for this are explained elsewhere. See, for example, the chapter titled "An Arabic Reciting: Qur'an as Spoken Book," in William A. Graham's, *Beyond the Written Word: Oral Aspects of Scripture in the History of Religion,* 79–115.

3. See 87:17. All references of this kind, with two numbers separated by a colon, are to the *Qu'ran.* The first number refers to chapter *(Surah)* and the second to verse *(Ayat).*

4. See 38:27.

## CHAPTER 2: THE SELF THAT SPEAKS

1. Sura 20:14. In the Torah, God says: "I am that I am" (Exodus 3:14). (Quotations from the Bible—the Torah, Psalms, and Gospels—are taken mainly from *The Thomson Chain-Reference Bible: King James Version.*

2. See 21:30.

3. See 39:6.

4. See 10:19.

5. See 3:109.

6. 96:1.

7. 17:44.

8. The Prophet Muhammad said: "Whoever has seen me, has seen the Truth" (*Sahih Muslim,* IV, 1225). And Jesus said: "I am the way, the truth,

and the life" (John 14:6). Jesus also said: "He that has seen me has seen the Father" (John 14:9). Perfect submission to God as the Anointer transforms the self into the Anointed (*Hristos*).

9. Jesus said: "I am the door: by me if any man enter in, he shall be saved" (John 10:9).

10. Jesus said: "Thou knowest what is within myself, and I know not what is within Thy self"(5:116).

11. See 17:110.

12. 2:186.

13. 33:72.

14. 2:31.

CHAPTER 3: THE WORLD

1. See 7:156.

2. *Sahih Muslim*, IV, 1437.

3. Ibid, 1438.

4. This tradition is central to the present discussion, and has many parallels in the verses of the Recitation: hence its essence is corroborated by sacred teaching. Although taken up and often repeated in the narratives and writings of well-known gnostic teachers, however, the tradition does not form part of the generally recognized collections of the Prophet Muhammad's sayings. For more on this see Chittick, *The Sufi Path*, 391n14 and, in particular, 250–52.

5. If asked how he knew about God, Abu Said al-Haraz would reply: "Through the fact that He brings opposites together." Ibn al-'Arabi frequently cites this assertion. See Chittick, *The Sufi Path*, 67, 115–16, 375.

6. The Prophet says: "His veil is the light. If He withdraws it, the splendour of His Face would consume His creation so far as His sight reaches" (*Sahih Muslim*, I, 113). Muhammad al-Ghazali quotes this saying in his *Mishkat*, along with the tradition that begins: "God has seventy or seventy thousand veils." Muhyiddin Ibn al-'Arabi frequently quotes this in his *al-Futuhat al-makkiyya*. See Chittick, *The Sufi Path*, 401n19.

7. See 3:83.

8. See 57:1, 59:1, 61:1.

9. Since this narrative is connected with the language of the Recitation, it should be made clear that its central terms of debt—submission, faith and goodness correspond to the Arabic *din—islam*, *iman* and *ihsan*.

10. 22:18.

11. A mosque (*masjid*, or "place of worship") is a place chosen or constructed for the expression of *sajda*: prostration, worship, submission. Whether natural or built, it may take various forms. The oldest mosque is *al-masjid al-haram*, the "Inviolable Mosque." The Recitation also speaks of mosques that differ from the "Inviolable," referring to *al-masjid al-aqsa*

or the "Further Mosque" and "places of worship" in the houses of the Israelites in Egypt (Sura 10:87) and above the Sleepers' Cave (18:21). *Masjid* (from which the word mosque derives) derives from the verb *sajada* ("to prostrate oneself," "to perform prostration"). The verbal form of the Semitic root *s-j-d* is common to majority of Aramaic dialects and means "to bow down, to prostrate oneself, to fall down, to perform the prostration, to pray, to serve." The earliest evidence of the term is in fact a loan word from the Akkadian *sagittu*, where it probably means "priestess," "attendant" (the feminine form of the Aramaic past participle). The earliest use of the term is to be found in a surviving Aramaic account on papyrus of Ashiqar, from the Elephantine islands, dating from the Achaemenian period, c. fifth century BCE, which reads:"Then did I, Ashiqar, indeed bow down and perform the prostration before Esarhaddon [king] of Assyria." The verb appears a number of times in the Aramaic section of the Old Testament Book of Daniel (2:46, 3:10 etc.) from the second century BCE (with in this case a statue as the object of the verb). The first use of the nominal form *msgd'* is found in one of the Elephantine papyri (late fifth century BCE): "With the oath sworn by Menahem, son of Shallum . . . shall oath be sworn to Meshullam, son of Nathan, H[erem] [God] in the masjid [*bmsgd'*] and Anath YHW." The precise meaning of *msgd'* in this case is not clear, but it is obviously an object that served as a sign of bowing down or prostration. This is the only known use in Achaemenian Aramaic. The noun is subsequently found in a small number of Nabataean records, most of which are from the Damascus and Basra regions and date from the first century CE, some of them given precise dates. These usually take the form: "This is the *msgd'* made by N for [the designated] God." These inscriptions are placed on stele. A number of second and third century CE Latin inscriptions set up by soldiers from the Commagen region refer to *Jupiter Turmasgadas*, which is the same vocalization as the Arabic *Turmasgide*. A Greek inscription from Dura Europos has a similar designation: "to Zeus Helios Mithras, the holy, the all-high, he who listens, Tourmasgate."

12. John 2:19. On language and meaning of the Further Mosque in relationships between human being and totality of created worlds, see also in Jalalu'ddin Rumi, *The Mathnawi*, 293–94, 298–99, 333–35, 343–44, 348–49.

13. 39:10.

## CHAPTER 4: HUMANKIND

1. *Sahih al-Bukhari*, VII, 336–37.

2. 41:53.

3. See 95:4. The Bosnian equivalent of "in the fairest stature" (the Qur'anic *fi ahsin takwīmin*) is *u najljepšoj uspravljenosti*: "in the most beautiful verticality" or "uprightness." As this more clearly reflects the

human person's esoteric role as the vertical axis which links the individual self to God through all the horizontal worlds, "verticality" or "uprightness" is often used to translate *uspravljenost(i)* in this essay.

4. See 33:21.
5. Ibn al-'Arabi, *al-Futuhat al-makkiyya*, III, 430.18.
6. 33:21.

## CHAPTER 5: THE BOOK

1. 22:70.
2. 13:38–39.
3. 10:47.
4. 5:48.
5. 14:4.
6. 30:22.
7. 31:27.
8. 6:59.
9. See 57:25.
10. See 26:193–94 and 16:102.
11. 42:52.
12. See 3:19.
13. 41:37.

## CHAPTER 6: DIGNITY

1. 7:172.
2. 58:7.
3. See 15:29.
4. The Arabīc *al-din ul-qayyim* means both "right religion" (as in most English translations of Sura 30:30–31) or "enduring debt" (as in the Bosnian version).
5. 30:30–31.
6. *Sahih Muslim*, IV, 1397.
7. See 41:34.
8. See 3:30.
9. See 49:13.
10. See 2: 187.
11. See 24:27–29.

## CHAPTER 7: ARRIVAL AND RETURN

1. See 6:163.
2. See 59:23.
3. See 112:3.

4. 2:156.

5. 45:13.

6. John 8:42.

7. John 8:54.

8. 39:11–12. This commandment from God, like the entire example of the Messenger, points to a social order that is not based on ruling people, but on submission between them in the Name of God. This is suggested, too, by Jesus' teachings: "The kings of the Gentiles exercise lordship over them; and they that exercise authority upon them are called benefactors. But ye shall not be so: but he that is greatest among you, let him be as the younger; and he that is chief, as he that doth serve." (Luke 22:25–26).

9. John 13:16.

10. John 13:20.

11. Sura 3:31.

12. John 14:21.

13. This descent and ascent corresponds to the two mosques of primal significance—the First or the Inviolable in the Valley (*al-masjid al-harām*) and the Second or the Further on the Mount (*al-masjid al-aqsa*). Located as we are at the very base of the arc of descent, we are the sum of all things from beginning to end; we are first in intention and last in manifestation. The direction we take begins from the Inviolable Mosque or being that which comes to rest and reaches the Remote Mosque or return to Peace. At the start of our return, our supreme potential is being the Light-giving Beacon (33:46) that receives his light from God as the Light of the heavens and the earth (24:35). At the end, or in full unicity, the Beacon is the same as the Light. From the human perspective, from the Valley, the Inviolable Mosque is the first or the start of the ascent, and the Further Mosque is the second, or the acme of human realization: the place where everything begins is also the end, and vice versa—in remoteness lies also proximity. The Inviolable Mosque is in the Vale of Tears, or at the base of creation, where it was erected when mankind's fall reached its ultimate depths. The building of the Mosque denotes a turning point: once the soul has experienced hell, it purifies itself and embarks on the return, which is the renewed bond with and ascent in the Intellect. (The central Cube, or Ka'ba, of the Inviolable Mosque is "clad" in black, the color of mourning, while the dome of the Further Mosque, the Dome of the Rock, is gilded.) The summit or goal of return is realization in the Intellect and union with God through it. This reversal at the bottom of the Valley and turning to the Intellect marks the axis linking the mosques—the Inviolable Mosque in the Valley and the Further Mosque on the Mount. These two extremities, designated by the two mosques, encompass the entire potential of the human self, from darkness to light, from the lowest of the low to the utmost rectitude. The name of the city where the mosque of return is located itself comprises what it denotes—City of Peace. God is Peace, and the return is to Him. The one who

returns is making the journey to Peace (*muslim*), and that to which the return is made is Peace (*as-Salam*). The journey of the seeker is making peace (*al-islam*); and the return to the heart, as the Long-enduring House (52:4) and the Abode of Peace (6:127, 10:25). "And yet doesn't popular piety also say that, at the end of time, the Ka'ba will come as a bride to the Dome of the Rock in Jerusalem?" (Annemarie Schimmel, *My Soul Is a Woman: The Feminine in Islam*, 101).

    14. 42:11.
    15. See 57:4.
    16. See 50:16.

## CHAPTER 8: SPACE

    1. 2:144.
    2. 17:1.
    3. 'Abd al-Razzaq Kashani, *al-Ta'wilat* (*Ta'wil al Qur'an*), I, 705–706. (Work published as *Tafsir al-Qur'an al-karim* and wrongly attributed to Ibn al-'Arabi.)
    4. 112:1–4.
    5. See 55:29.

## CHAPTER 9: TIME

    1. 30:18.
    2. 4:103.
    3. 2:238. For the reason for selecting this translation, see Muhammad Asad, *The Message of the Qur'an*, 53.
    4. See 18:28.
    5. See 11:114.
    6. See 50:39–40.
    7. See 17:78.
    8. Ibid.
    9. See 73:20.
    10. See 62:9.
    11. See 73:20.
    12. 16:90.
    13. 2:272.
    14. 2:177.
    15. 2:184–85.
    16. See 2:187.
    17. The reflection between Sun and Moon is echoed in Bosnian by the close relationship between the words *Um* ("Intellect") and *Razum* ("Reason").
    18. 3:96–97.

19. 2:189.
20. 2:197.
21. See continuation of 2:197.
22. 22:27–28.

CHAPTER 10: NATURE

1. 7:40.
2. 2:222.
3. 4:135.
4. 91:7–10.
5. 15:21–23.
6. 23:71.

CHAPTER 11: THE OPENING

1. *Al-Fātihā*, the opening chapter of the Qur'an.

CHAPTER 12: THE DEBT

1. See *Sahih Muslim*, I, 1–3.
2. See 53:14.
5. 31:14.

CHAPTER 13: POVERTY

1. 4:48.
2. 47:38.
3. *Sahih al-Bukhari*, IV, 140. See Chittick, *The Sufi Path,* 395n17.
4. See 2:177.
5. 22:36–37
6. Referring to those who seek salvation, the Messiah, Jesus son of Mary, calls for the denial of the self for the sake of the Self, and for this denial to be realized in himself as the Word. He says (Matthew 16:25): "For whosoever will save his life shall lose it: and whosoever will lose his life for my sake shall find it." This is because the Self alone is life.
7. 90:12–16.
8. *Sahih Muslim,* IV, 1363. See Chittick, *The Sufi Path*, 292n33, and William A. Graham, *The Divine Word and Prophetic Word in Early Islam,* 178–80.
9. 102:1–3.

CHAPTER 14: MARY

1. 3:37.
2. When the angel Gabriel announced to the Virgin Mary the message from God that she would conceive and give birth to a son as His Word, she

replied: "Behold the handmaid of the Lord: be it unto me according to Thy word" (Luke 1:38).

3. 66:12.

4. 3:42–43. The Praiser says in one of his traditions that Mary, along with Asiya, Khadija and Fatima, is one of the four best women who ever lived. See Ahmad ibn Hanbal, *al-Musnad*, III, 135, and J. D. McAuliffe, "Chosen of all women: Mary and Fatima in Qur'anic exegesis," *Islamochristiana*, VII, 1981, 19–28.

5. 3:45.

6. 19:24–26.

7. *Sahih al-Bukhari*, VIII, 106.

8. 23:50.

9. 5:114–15.

## CHAPTER 15: "PURIFY MY HOUSE"

1. *Sahih al-Bukhari*, IV, 383, and *Sahih Muslim*, I, 264. For more on the connection between the Holy Mosque and Adam, see *The History of Al-Tabari*, I, *General Introduction* and *From the Creation to the Flood*, 293–95.

2. *Sahih al-Bukhari*, IV, 383 and *Sahih Muslim*, I, 264. For more on the connection between the Prophet Abraham and the Holy Mosque, see also Martin Lings, *Muhammad: His Life Based on the Earliest Sources*, 1–3; and Ibn Ishaq, *Sirat Rasul Allah (The Life of Muhammad)*, 45.

3. In Arabic *al-masjid al-harām*, i.e. the Inviolable Mosque—a meaning which is kept in the Bosnian equivalent *Zabranjeni mesdžid*.

4. 22:26–27; and see 2:125.

5. 2:127–29.

6. See 53:37.

7. See 60:4, 6.

8. See 17:2–7.

9. See John 2:14–21, which recounts how Jesus drove out the sellers of oxen and sheep and doves and the money changers from the temple of Jerusalem with a scourge. His disciples recognized in this the words of the Psalms: "The zeal of thine house hath eaten me up" (Psalms 69:10). This passage from the Gospels denotes the oneness of the mosque and the inner human self. Maccabees II (5:19–20) explains: "The Lord, however, had not chosen the people for the sake of the Place, but the Place for the sake of the people [ . . . ] and what the Almighty had forsaken in his anger was restored in all its glory, once the great Sovereign became reconciled."

10. *Sahih Muslim*, I, 105.

## CHAPTER 16: THE ASCENSION

1. 2:144.

2. *Sahih Muslim*, I, 265.

3. 28:88.
4. 112:1.
5. See 53:14–18.
6. See 52:4.
7. Sura 22:40. It must be stressed that different interpretations are possible of this verse, though they are crucial for this study. One interpretation identifies the four places of worship in the verse with the four principles of nature (earth, air, water and fire); another with angels. However, of these four different forms "within which God's name has been mentioned often", the first three (monasteries/*sawami'*, churches/*biya'*, synagogues/*salawat*) may also be seen as stages on the way to the fourth, the innermost core (mosques/*masajid*).

The first stage is *sawami'* (monasteries). The verb *s-w-m*, from which the noun *sawami'* is derived, means "being with peace" or "turning to peace." (From the same semantic root, which corresponds to the verb "to fast," the noun "fasting" is derived.) The duality of all that is created calls to the oneness of peace. By withdrawing from the lower levels of existence, an enlightened human being can ascend toward the higher levels, toward his or her covenant with God. As humans, once we recognize the duality between this world and the other, and once we accept the latter as the higher and more superior, we can begin to move from this world toward the higher. In so doing, we grow closer to Peace as Oneness; we become ready to hatch new life from the egg of the world, to be reborn in and with the spirit. Our human journey through this universe takes us ever further from the lower world and ever closer to the Spirit, so that we may die in order to be born anew. By seeing the external world so clearly, by becoming aware of the world, we come to question ourselves as human beings, and thus turn away from the external world toward the inner self.

The external world then becomes a journey toward the inner world, toward self-gained knowledge. This is the second stage, as signified by *biya'* (churches). Research has shown that the word *biya'* derives from the word "egg" (Syriac *bi'ta*). In turning toward the self, humans gain knowledge of their original nature.

In being reborn, in rediscovering our original nature, we renew our original covenant with God. Hence we reconcile our will with the Will of God. Our will turns us toward God, connecting us with Him through love and knowledge. This is the third stage of the journey. It is signified by the noun *salawat,* which is usually translated as "synagogues" or "oratories". In its verbal root one may recognize the Aramaic *sl'*, with its primal meaning of "to connect," "to bow," and "to worship."

Along these three stages of the journey, the traveler becomes transformed into submission to God. This is the meaning of "mosques" (*masajid*): our openness toward the Light of the Intellect, toward the praise which connects us with the Lord of the Lights of the Worlds. These places are revealed through all the numberless forms, for which the "mosque" is both beginning and end, inner and outer. This journey follows the upright way, in perfect harmony between human will and God's Will. It leads toward the heart, which lies between the two fingers of God. Our highest potential as humans is that of full submission to God and to His Will. When we achieve this, we are "in" the mosque and we "are" the mosque—that is, we are ready to receive the names given to us by God. In so doing, human beings manifest themselves as the totality of creation. All the worlds are collected in a human being. Both are included in the same submission to God.

8. 3:64.

9. For more on the languages and meanings of church, synagogue and mosque, see Titus Burckhardt, *Art of Islam: Language and Meaning*; Burckhardt, *Sacred Art in East and West: Its Principles and Methods*; Burckhardt, *Chartres and the Birth of the Cathedral*; Martin Lings, "The Symbolism of the Mosque and the Cathedral in the Life of the Stations of Wisdom," in *Symbol & Archetype: A Study of the Meaning of Existence*, 113–36; Leo Schaya, "The Meaning of the Temple," in *The Sword of Gnosis: Metaphysics, Cosmology, Tradition, Symbolism*, 359–65.

## Chapter 17: The Holy

1. 2:1–2.

## Chapter 18: The Name

1. See 2:31.

2. 17:110.

3. 57:4.

4. 70:1–4.

5. Titus Burckhardt, *Introduction aux Doctrines ésotériques de l'Islam*, 101.

## Chapter 19: The Peace

1. See 2:144, 149, 150.

2. Traditions of this nature are often cited by Ibn al-ʿArabi in his work *al-Futuhat al-makiyya*. See Chittick, *The Sufi Path*, 389 n.6.

3. When asked where God was, the Messenger said: "In the hearts of His faithful servants." (Tradition quoted in Muhammad al-Ghazali, *Ihya' ulum al-din*, III, 1328.) This is also related to the tradition: "My heavens and My earth embrace Me not, but the heart of My believing servant does

embrace Me." This tradition is familiar to gnostics, though it was not possible to ascertain the chain of transmission. (See Chittick, *The Sufi Path*, 396n20).

4. See 89:27–30.

5. 5:16.

6. 19:58. See also 17:108–110.

7. 97:3–4.

# Bibliography

Arberry, Arthur. *The Koran Interpreted*. London: George Allen & Unwin, 1980.

Asad, Muhammad. *The Message of the Qur'an*. Gibraltar: Dar al-Andalus, 1980.

Bukhari, Imam al-. *Sahih al-Bukhari*, transl. Muhammad Muhsin Khan. Beirut: Dar al Arabia, 1985.

Burckhardt, Titus. *Introduction aux Doctrines ésotériques de l'Islam*. Paris: Dervy-Livres, 1969.

———. *Art of Islam: Language and Meaning*, transl. J. Peter Hobson. London: World of Islam Festival Publishing Company, 1976.

———. *Sacred Art in East and West: Its Principles and Methods*, transl. Lord Northbourne. Pates Manor: Perennial Books, 1986.

———. *Chartres and the Birth of the Cathedral,* transl. William Stoddart. Cambridge: Golgonooza Press, 1995.

Chittick, William C. *The Sufi Path of Knowledge: Ibn al-'Arabi's Metaphysics of Imagination*. Albany: State University of New York Press, 1989.

Ghazali, Muhammad, al-. *Ihya' ulum al-din*. Beirut: Dar al-Arabia, s.a.

———. *The Niche of Lights*, transl. David Buchman. Provo: Brigham Young University Press, 1989.

Graham, William A. *The Divine Word and Prophetic Word in Early Islam*. The Hague: Mouton, 1977.

———. *Beyond the Written Word: Oral Aspects of Scripture in the History of Religion*. Cambridge: Cambridge University Press, 2001.

Ibn al-'Arabi. *al-Futuhat al-makkiyya*. Beirut: Dar Sadir.

Ibn Hanbal, Ahmad. *al-Musnad*. Beirut: Dar Sadir.

Ibn Ishaq. *Sirat Rasul Allah (The Life of Muhammad)*, transl. Alfred Guillaume. Karachi: Oxford University Press, 1980.

Kashani, 'Abd al-Razzaq. *al-Ta'wilat (Ta'wil al Qur'an)*. Beirut: Dar al-Yaqzat al-Adabiyya, 1968.

Lings, Martin. *Muhammad: His Life Based on Earliest Sources*. London: Unwin, 1988.

————. *Symbol and Archetipe: A Study of the Meaning of Existence*. Cambridge: Quinta Essentia, 1991.

McAuliffe, J. D. "Chosen of All Women: Mary and Fatima in Qur'anic Exegesis," *Islamochristiana*, VII, 1981, 19–28.

Muslim, Imam. *Sahih Muslim*. Translated by Abdul Hamid Siddiqi. Riyadh: International Islamic Publishing House.

Rumi, Jalalu'ddin. *The Mathnawi*. Translated by Reynold A. Nicholson. London: Luzac, 1977.

Schaya, Leo. "The Meaning of the Temple." In *The Sword of Gnosis: Metaphysics. Cosmology, Tradition, Symbolism*, ed. Jacob Needleman. London: Arkana, 1986.

Schimmel, Annemarie. *My Soul Is a Woman: The Feminine in Islam*. London: The Continuum International Publishing Group, 1997.

*The History of Al-Tabari*. Translated by Franz Rosenthal. Albany: State University of New York Press, 1989.

*The Thompson Chain-Reference Bible: King James Version*. Fifth Improved Edition. Indianapolis: B. B. Kirkbride Bible Company, 1988.

# Index